U0937893

"十二五"职业教育国家规划教材
经全国职业教育教材审定委员会审定

高职高专经管类核心课教改项目成果系列规划教材
教育部高职高专英语类专业教指委精品课程配套教材

外贸函电实操

（第二版·增订版）

朱佩珍　徐腾飞　主编
应纯艳　潘百翔　张　康　副主编
杨　艳　主审

科学出版社
北　京

内 容 简 介

随着我国对外贸易的不断发展，旧有的函电方式已经无法满足外贸行业新的需求。为使本书适应行业发展及教学新形势的需要，编者在广泛征求各相关院校及外贸行业从业人员意见的基础上，对之前的版本进行了修订。本次修订吸纳了行业资深人士的建议和意见，在如下三个方面进行了创新和较大改动：①变单元为学习情境，以目前极具代表性的三种贸易方式，即一般贸易、加工贸易和外贸代理作为载体来设计学习情境；②内容上，更新询盘、报盘、签约、装运、支付等各个外贸环节的知识背景；③根据国际、国内贸易规则变化及商务交流沟通方式等的新变化，将书中原有冗长、过时的内容删除，添加新的知识信息、写作技巧、例函、术语等。

本书可作为高职高专外贸专业的教学用书，亦可供外贸行业从事人员阅读。

图书在版编目（CIP）数据

外贸函电实操/朱佩珍，徐腾飞主编. —2版. —北京：科学出版社，2016
（“十二五”职业教育国家规划教材・高职高专经管类核心课教改项目成果系列规划教材）

ISBN 978-7-03-047843-6

Ⅰ.①外… Ⅱ.①朱… ②徐… Ⅲ.①对外贸易—英语—电报信函—写作—高等职业教育—教材 Ⅳ.①H315

中国版本图书馆 CIP 数据核字（2016）第 053397 号

责任编辑：李 娜 朱大益/责任校对：王万红
责任印制：吕春珉/封面设计：子时文化

科学出版社出版

北京东黄城根北街 16 号
邮政编码：100717
http://www.sciencep.com

北京九州迅驰传媒文化有限公司 印刷

科学出版社发行 各地新华书店经销

*

2010 年 6 月第 一 版 开本：787×1092 1/16
2016 年 3 月第 二 版 印张：12 1/4
2020 年 7 月第二版增订版 字数：288 000
2021 年 3 月第九次印刷

定价：37.00 元

（如有印装质量问题，我社负责调换〈九州迅驰〉）

销售部电话 010-62136230 编辑部电话 010-62138978-2018

高职高专经管类核心课教改项目成果系列规划教材

编写指导委员会

Foreword

本书在编写思路上较同类教材有较大的突破，以贸易方式为载体设计学习情境，挑选目前具有代表性的三种贸易方式，即一般贸易、加工贸易和外贸代理作为载体来设计学习情境。开篇即引入企业实际案例，旨在培养学生把外贸英语函电写作融入常见业务案例的实践操作能力。全书共分为三大学习情境和七个子情境，分别为一般贸易中的小商品出口贸易、电动工具出口贸易和纺织品出口贸易，加工贸易中的来料加工和进料加工，以及外贸代理中的一般代理和独家代理。在每个情境内容的组织上，按照外贸从业人员，尤其是外贸业务员的成长历程以及学生认知能力培养规律来组织，子情境的设置同样从简单到复杂，让学生在比较学习中，不断提高其外贸函电的写作技能。如：第一个情境即一般贸易中，第一个子情境被设置为协助公司有经验的业务员开展外贸业务，目的是培养学生外贸业务的操作能力；第二个子情境设计为业务员开始独立开拓市场，目的是培养学生独立开展外贸业务的能力；第三个子情境设计为外贸业务员独立处理外贸业务中出现的各种问题，目的是培养学生熟练开展外贸业务的能力。三大子学习情境之间呈递进关系，难度逐步增加。

三大学习情境涉及的外贸业务从初级到高级。不同学习情境采用不同企业的业务案例，使学生在接触不同企业业务操作方法的同时，熟悉更多的产品知识，接触不同的写作风格，实现书本知识与外贸实际业务的零距离对接，强化外贸英语函电的实践过程，更加适合高职高专学生和外贸工作从事者学习和使用。

本书由朱佩珍副教授、徐腾飞副教授担任主编，杨艳教授担任主审。各学习情境编写分工如下：学习情境一由朱佩珍、董乓、吴亚琴、姚娜、张燕编写；学习情境二由朱佩珍、徐腾飞、胡艳艳编写；学习情境三由应纯艳、潘百翔、张康编写。朱佩珍、应纯艳、杨艳进行了全书的统稿和审定。

本书编写过程中，得到了许多热心人士的支持，尤其是合作企业外贸人员的鼎力协助，在此向他们表示衷心的感谢！

限于编者的水平和时间，书中阙误之处在所难免，殷切希望广大读者不吝赐教，以便再版时进一步修订与完善。

Contents

Study Situation 1

1.1 Small Commodities Export Transaction

Business Background:

浙江欣欣饰品有限公司地处义乌市，成立于1990年，公司专业生产并出口银饰品。最近该公司收到美国老客户 Sun Trading Co., Ltd.的询盘，作为公司业务助理，你要协助业务员进行贸易磋商，签订合同，最终顺利完成出口业务。

Business Requirements:

1. 熟悉公司情况和饰品信息，尤其是时尚戒指。
2. 了解商务函电的格式、写作原则等。
3. 能够根据客户询盘撰写报盘函。
4. 能够根据订单起草合同，撰写签约函。
5. 能够落实预付款，撰写付款函。
6. 可以根据对方对包装的要求撰写包装函。
7. 会撰写装运函，并寄出装船单据。
8. 能够撰写业务善后函。

Teaching Objective:

通过协助有经验的业务员开展外贸业务，培养外贸业务的实际操作能力。

Company Profile

Zhejiang Xinxin Ornament Co., Ltd. established in 1990 and located in Yiwu City is a manufacturer and exporter of sterling silver fashion jewelry with designing and wholesaling. There are more than 500 employees, including 50 professional design staff. The products are being exported to clients in Europe, North America and Asia.

We specialize in 925 sterling silver jewelry, brass jewelry, and jewelry containing semi-precious stones, of which we have many years of experience on production and marketing. The main products include necklaces, bracelets, rings, earrings, toe rings, bangles, brooches and tie clips, currently offering over 15 000 styles.

The company can also do the international business on OEM[1] & ODM[2] basis. New product development, customer-oriented items, timely delivery and technical service are all handled by professionals. Prompt response will be guaranteed. With the principle of "Quality First", we are confident that our competitive prices and attentive service will be sure to meet your expectations.

Our 23 years' production experience, strong R&D[3] capability and comprehensive after-sales service will be of great help to you both in marketing and consultation. You are warmly welcome anytime to visit our company.

For more information about our company or products, please feel free to contact us. Your satisfaction is our greatest success.

Task 1 Inquiry and Offer

Writing Background

林枫是浙江欣欣饰品有限公司新入职的外贸业务员，公司安排其担任高级业务员李宁的助理，在半年的实习期内，协助李宁完成外贸业务。

近日李宁收到了美国老客户 Sun Trading Co., Ltd.的下列询盘：

Dear Mr. Li,

We are much impressed by your Fasion Finger Rings series, especially Type1001, 1002, 1003 and 1004. We would be appreciated if you could quote us your best prices on CIF New York all including 3% commission.

Waiting for your reply!

Yours Truly,
Sun Trading Co., Ltd.
Smith Johnson
Purchasing Division

Writing Task

请根据上述背景资料，以欣欣饰品公司外贸业务员李宁的名义，给 Sun Trading Co., Ltd. 去函，对询盘进行回复，并对询盘中提及的四款产品进行报盘。

Writing Guide

The written mode of communication has always been popular as it generally provides a more permanent record of the messages transmitted. This mode of communication consists of a variety of media, e.g. letters, e-mails, faxes, etc., among which e-mails are the most frequently used media.

E-mail is of crucial importance in the conduct of business activities. It plays an essential role in a company's correspondence with the clients.

1. The Structure of Business Letter

A business letter consists of seven necessary parts: the letter-head, the date, the inside name and address, the salutation, the body, the complimentary close and the signature. When appropriate, any of the following optional parts can be included: reference number, subject line, enclosure, carbon copy, postscript and Attention Line.

(1)Necessary Parts

1) Letter head（信头）

The letter-head expresses a firm's personality. It helps to give the client the first impression of the writer's firm. Usually printed, a letter-head may include the firm's name, address, post code, telephone numbers, fax number, e-mail address and even a symbol of the firm.

2) Date（日期）

Always type the date in full. The following is four forms of expression:

24th July, 2010	July 24th, 2010
24 July, 2010	July 24, 2010

To give the day in figures (e.g. 11/9/2010) is informal, and it may easily cause confusion because in Britain this date would mean 11th September 2010, but in the United States and some other countries it would mean 9th November 2010.

3) Inside Name and Address（信内名称和地址）

The inside name and address are typed below the date, next to the left-hand margin. The major function is to provide the writer with a record of to whom and where the letter will be sent. The inside name and address of a letter to an individual consist the person's courtesy title, name, business or executive title and address, while to a group, the inside name and address includes the full group name and address.

The courtesy title used in correspondence contains Mr., Mrs., Miss and Messrs., and Mrs. is used for a married woman and Miss is for a used single woman. In recent years, it has become customary to use Ms. as the courtesy title for all women, married or unmarried. Messrs., the plural form of Mr., is used only for companies or firms, the name of which includes a personal element, e.g. Messrs. G. Johnson & Co.

4) Salutation（称呼）

The salutation is the greeting with which every letter begins. The customary greeting in business letter is Dear Sir or Dear Sirs, but Americans usually use Gentlemen instead of Dear Sirs. If the writer is not sure whether the letter will be read by a man or a woman, please use the greeting Dear Madam or Sir. If the writer knows the name of the reader, please use the greeting Dear Mr.×××, or Dear ×××.

5) Body（正文）

A body, where all the information is to be given, is the part that really matters. Before you begin to write, you must first of all consider the following points:

① What is your aim to write this letter?

② What is the best way to go about it?

The body must state the aim of the letter, and it should be easily understood. The following serves as reminders:

① Use simple, clear, courteous, grammatical words, and write to the point;

② Paragraph correctly, confining each paragraph to one topic;

③ Avoid stereotyped phrases and commercial jargons.

6) Complimentary Close（信尾敬语）

The complimentary close, like the salutation, is purely a matter of custom and a polite way of bringing a letter to a close. The expression used must suit the occasion. It must also match the salutation.

Dear Sir (s)/ Dear Madam ⟶ Yours Faithfully/Truly, Faithfully Yours

Gentlemen ⟶ Yours truly, Truly yours, Yours sincerely

Dear Mr. Wang ⟶ Yours sincerely

Dear Helen ⟶ Best Wishes/Best Regards

7) Signature（签名）

The signature is the signed name or mark of the person writing the letter or that of the firm he or she represents. It is written in ink immediately after the complimentary close. To "sign" with a rubber stamp is a form of discourtesy. If the writer is on behalf of his company, the signature includes the following points:

① The name of the company;

② The name of the signer;

③ The position of the signer.

(2) Optional Parts

1) Reference Number（参考号）

The function of a reference number is to designate the numbers of the relevant letters when writing for the purpose of consulting and filing.

Frequently used expressions: Your ref./ Our ref..

2) Subject Line（主题行）

The subject line is regarded as a part of the body of a business letter. Usually it is in the upper case or initial capitals/underline and placed between the salutation and the body of a letter to call attention to what content the letter is about.

Frequently used expressions: Re:/Subject:/Sub:.

e.g. Subject: Our Quotation Sheet No. 123

3) Enclosure（附件）

An enclosure can be anything in the envelope in addition to the message itself.

It is typed two line spaces after the signature when something is sent along with the letter.

If the enclosures are more than one, the number should be marked.

Frequently used abbreviations：Enc., Encs..

e.g. Enc.: a price list.

4) Carbon Copy（C.C.）（抄送）

If you want to give a copy to other persons besides the addressee, you should type the names of these persons after Carbon Copy（C.C.）below everything else typed on the page.

e.g. C.C.: Mr. Franklin

5) Postscript（P.S.）（附言）

When you find something forgotten to be included in the letter body before the envelope being sealed up, you may state it after the signature in a postscript with a simple signature again. The adding of a P.S. should, however, be avoided as far as possible.

e.g. P.S.: The shipping advice concerning the said goods will be sent to you by fax on July 7.

6) Attention Line（经办人提示行）

An attention line is considered a part of the inside address and it leads the letter to a particular person or department when the letter is addressed to a company. It is usually between the inside address and the salutation or above the inside address.

e.g. For the attention of Mr. Rawls; Attention：Export Department.

Fig.1.1 shows a sample of the layout of a business letter:

Letter Head

Date

Inside Name & Address

Attention Line

Salutation

Subject Line

Body ______________________________

Complimentary Close

Signature

Enc.

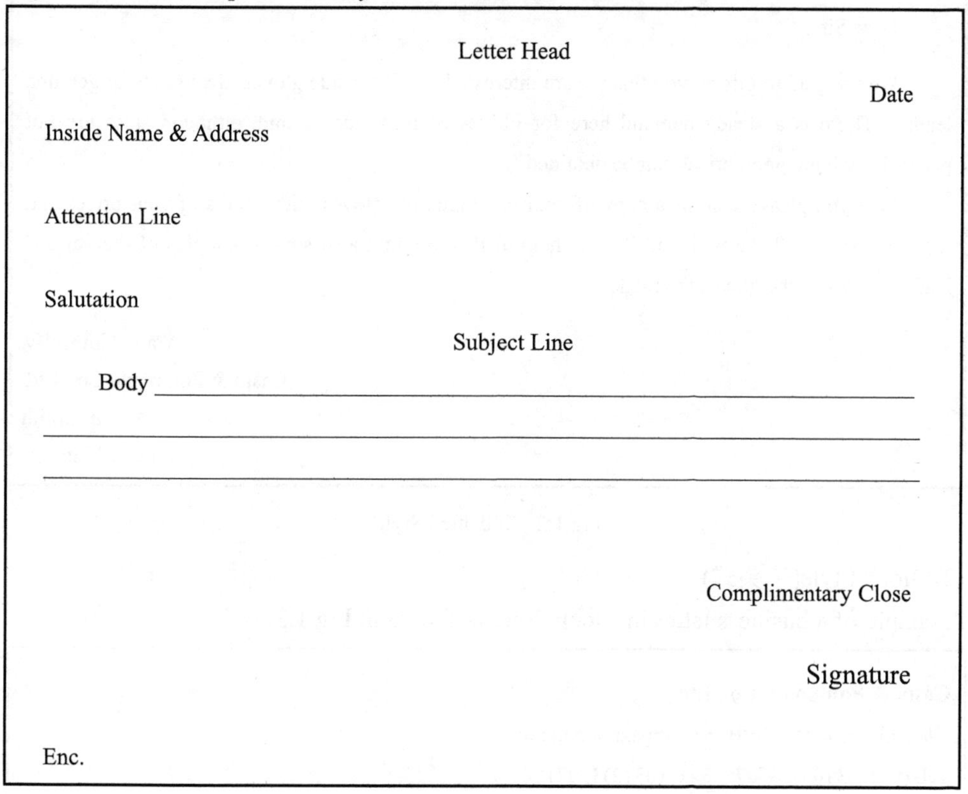

Fig.1.1 The Layout of a Business Letter

2. The Style of Business Letter

Generally speaking, there are four styles in business letter writing, namely, Indented Style, Block Style, Semi-block Style and Simplified Style.

Please study the four styles by reading the samples of business letters as follows.

(1) Indented Style(缩进式)

A sample of a business letter in Indented Style is shown in Fig.1.2.

Casio & Pomponia Co., Ltd.
Ulucanlar Caddesi 36/B, Samanpazari, Ankara
Tel: (0312)3104109-07   Fax: (0312)3102106-17
E-mail: onbirller@ttbet.net.tr

November 10, 2008

Si Fang Holding Group
No.234, Chouzhou Road, Yiwu City,
Zhejiang Province, China

Dear Sirs,

We are glad to inform you that we are interested in hand-made gloves in a variety of genuine leather. There is a steady demand here for gloves of high quality and, although sales are not particularly high, good prices can be obtained.

Will you please send us a copy of your catalogue for gloves with details of your prices and terms of payment? We will find it most helpful if you could also supply samples of the various leather of which the gloves are made.

Yours Faithfully,
Casio & Pomponia Co., Ltd.
Mr. Smith
General Manager

Fig.1.2 Indented Style

(2) Block Style(平头式)

A sample of a business letter in Block Style is shown in Fig.1.3.

Casio & Pomponia Co., Ltd.
Ulucanlar Caddesi 36/B, Samanpazari, Ankara
Tel: (0312)3104109-07   Fax: (0312)3102106-17
E-mail: onbirller@ttbet.net.tr

Fig.1.3 Block Style

November 10, 2008

Si Fang Holding Group
No.234, Chouzhou Road, Yiwu City,
Zhejiang Province, China

Dear Sirs,

We are glad to inform you that we are interested in hand-made gloves in a variety of genuine leather. There is a steady demand here for gloves of high quality and, although sales are not particularly high, good prices can be obtained.

Will you please send us a copy of your catalogue for gloves with details of your prices and terms of payment? We will find it most helpful if you could also supply samples of the various leather of which the gloves are made.

Yours Faithfully,
Casio & Pomponia Co., Ltd.
Mr. Smith
General Manager

Fig.1.3 Block Style(continue)

(3) Semi-block Style(混合式)

A sample of a business letter in Semi-block Style is shown in Fig.1.4.

Casio & Pomponia Co., Ltd.
Ulucanlar Caddesi 36/B, Samanpazari, Ankara
Tel: (0312)3104109-07 Fax: (0312)3102106-17
E-mail: onbirller@ttbet.net.tr

November 10, 2008

Si Fang Holding Group
No.234, Chouzhou Road, Yiwu City,
Zhejiang Province, China

Dear Sirs,

We are glad to inform you that we are interested in hand-made gloves in a variety of genuine leather. There is a steady demand here for gloves of high quality and, although sales are not particularly high, good prices can be obtained.

Will you please send us a copy of your catalogue for gloves with details of your prices and terms

Fig.1.4 Semi-block Style

of payment? We will find it most helpful if you could also supply samples of the various leather of which the gloves are made.

Yours Faithfully,
Casio & Pomponia Co., Ltd.
Mr. Smith
General Manager

Fig.1.4 Semi-block Style(continue)

(4) Simplified Style (简化式)

Simplified style is often used in a fax and e-mail.

1) A sample of Fax Style (传真样本) is shown in Fig.1.5.

Heading (Sender's information)

From: Date:
To: Pages:
Attn:

Salutation
Body ______________________________
____

Complimentary Close
Signature

Fig.1.5 Fax Style

2) A sample of E-mail Style (邮件样本) is shown is Fig.1.6.

From: (发件人)	t-white@abc.com
Date: (日期)	31December, 2009, 11:24:30
To: (收件人)	b-smith@benton.com
Subject: (主题)	Order No. 456

Bob Smith, (称呼)
Body ______________________________
____

Yours,
White

Fig.1.6 E-mail Style

3. Writing Principles

When you write a business letter, you should follow the 7 "C"s: completeness, concreteness, clearness, conciseness, courtesy, consideration and correctness.

(1)Completeness (完整)

A business letter should include all the necessary information. It is essential to check the message carefully before it is sent out. Completeness means that all the matters are discussed and all the questions are answered.

(2)Concreteness (具体)

Make the message specific and definite.

e.g.Our oranges are of top quality.→Our oranges are juicy and sweet.

e.g.It is our big client.→It did more than two million worth of business with us last year.

(3)Clearness (清楚)

First of all, make sure that your letter is so clear that it cannot be misunderstood. A point that is ambiguous in a letter will cause trouble to both sides, and further exchange of letters for explanation will become inevitable. Thus time will be lost.

Next, when you are sure about what you want to say, say it in plain, simple words. Straightforward and simple words are needed in business letters and negotiations.

A letter can be made clearer, easier to read and more attractive by careful paragraphing. A paragraph for each point is a good rule.

(4)Conciseness (简洁)

A concise letter is not necessarily a short one. Sometimes a letter dealing perhaps with a multiplicity of matters cannot avoid being long. If conciseness conflicts with courtesy, then make a little sacrifice of conciseness. Generally speaking, you will gain in clearness and conciseness by writing short sentences rather than long ones.

(5)Courtesy (礼貌)

It should hardly be necessary to stress the importance of courtesy in your correspondence. One of the most important things is promptness. Punctuality will please your customer who dislikes waiting for days before he gets a reply to his letter.

The courteous writer should be sincere and tactful, thoughtful and appreciative.

(6)Consideration (周到)

Consideration emphasizes You-attitude rather than We-attitude. When writing a letter, keep the reader's requests, needs, desires as well as his feelings in mind. Plan the best way to present the message for the reader to receive.

(7)Correctness (正确)

Correctness refers to not only correct usage of grammar, punctuation and spelling, but also standard language, proper statement, accurate figures as well as correct understanding and using of commercial jargons.

4. Superscription

目前商务函电大多通过电子邮件或传真来发送，有时也可能采用邮寄的方式，因此有必要了解一下信封的写法。常见的信封样本如下：

Sender's name and address		(stamp) Registered
	Recipient's name and address	
Confidential (private)		

5. Inquiry

询盘是指交易的一方为购买或销售货物而向对方提出的有关交易条件的询问。询盘通常由买方发出，也可以由卖方发出。询盘分为一般询盘和具体询盘。

一般询盘（a general inquiry）：索取普通资料，如目录、价目表或报价单、样品、图片等。

具体询盘（a specific inquiry）：具体询问商品名称、规格、数量、单价、装船期、付款方式等。

询盘多为买方向卖方发出。买方通过询盘函，简明扼要地向卖方了解一般的商品信息。询盘函无需写得过分客气，只需具体、简洁、措辞得体。有的询盘函直截了当地说明订购打算，希望对方给予一定优惠条件；有的询盘函则以征询信息的方式，不承诺下单，以避免因未订购而可能形成的日后交易中的障碍。

首次询盘一般包括以下内容：

1）交代如何得知对方名称和地址；

2）简单介绍本公司以及公司经营的产品；

3）阐述该函电的目的，如对商品质量、数量、价格等方面的询问；

4）表达愿望，希望对方回复或报盘。

如果已经收到对方的建交函，则询盘函应包括以下内容：

1）感谢对方的来函；

2）阐述该函电的目的，如对商品质量、数量、价格等方面的询问；

3）希望对方给予回复。

An inquiry means a request for information. In foreign trade, an inquiry is usually made by the buyers without engagement to get information about the goods to be ordered, such as price, catalogue, samples, delivery date and other terms. Inquiries should be complete, brief, specific, courteous and reasonable. Generally, inquiries can be divided into general inquiries and specific inquiries. The former asks information about various goods; the latter asks information about some specific goods.

A "first inquiry", that is an inquiry sent to a supplier whom you have not previously dealt with, should begin by telling him how you obtained his name. Some details of your own business, such as the kind of goods handled, quantities needed, usual terms of trade and any information likely to enable the supplier to decide what he or she can do for you, will also help.

6. Reply

收到客户的询盘，即意味着一个潜在的交易成功机会，因此对客户的询盘要及时、礼貌、认真地予以回复，还要表明与对方合作的愿望，既促进合作又增进友谊。

A reply means the answer to inquiries. Replies should include the following points:

① State firstly how you appreciate it;

② Answer all the questions;

③ Hope to receive the order.

In case the goods inquired for are currently out of stock, the supplier should inform the inquirer when they will be available and, by taking this opportunity, introduce some other products as substitutes so as to create a good impression, which hopefully will result in more business.

Replies should be prompt, courteous and helpful.

7. Offer

发盘往往是发盘人在收到对方询盘后发出的，但也可在未收到询盘的情况下由发盘人直接对受盘人发出。实际外贸业务中，发盘大多由卖方发出。一项有效的发盘应该具备以下四个条件：

1）发盘必须向一个（或几个）特定受盘人提出（注意概念上要与“发盘邀请”相区别）。普通商业广告、商品目录、价目单等不能构成有效发盘，因为没有特定的对象，而只能视作邀请发盘。英美法系中规定：向公众作出的商业广告，只要内容明确，在某些场合下也视为发盘。大陆法系中规定：凡向公众发布的商业广告，不得视为发盘；《联合国国际货物销售合同公约》（以下简称《公约》）持折中态度，如带有“本广告构成发盘”或“将售予最先支付货款的公司”等字样也被视为发盘。

2）发盘的内容必须十分确定。如果内容不确定，即使对方接受，也不构成合同成立。

3）发盘必须明确表示发盘人受其约束。例如：①使用表示发盘的术语。如“发盘”“不可撤销发盘”“递盘”“不可撤销递盘”“订购”“订货”等。②明确规定有效期，如“……限××日复到有效”等内容。一项发盘通常包含商品的品质、数量、包装、价格、交货、付款六个主要方面的交易条件。《公约》第十四条规定：“……如果写明货物并且明示或暗示地规定数量和价格或规定如何确定数量和价格，即为十分确定。”如此来看，一项发盘只要包含商品的名称、数量、价格这三个要素，就算完整。若发盘中带有保留条件和限制性条件，如“仅供参考”“以我方最后确认为准”“以未售出为准”，此类发盘其实是虚盘，发盘人不受其约束。

4）发盘必须送达受盘人。根据《公约》规定，发盘于送达受盘人时生效。如发盘由于在传递中遗失以致受盘人未能收到，则该发盘无效。

An offer of goods is usually made by the seller in order to answer inquiries. Offers can be classified into firm offer（实盘）and non-firm offer（虚盘）. The difference between a firm offer and a non-firm offer is that a firm offer cannot be taken back by the exporter because of the time limit while a non-firm offer can be taken back at will. A firm offer is a promise to sell goods at a stated price, usually within a stated period of time. It must be clear, definite, complete and final.

In response to an inquiry, offers may be sent. A satisfactory offer will include the following:

① An expression of thanks for the inquiry;

② Details of prices, discounts and terms of payment;

③ A statement or clear indication of what the prices cover (e.g. freight and insurance, etc.);

④ An undertaking as to date of delivery or time of shipment;

⑤ The period for which the offer is valid;

⑥ An expression of hope that the offer will be accepted.

Reference E-mail

Dear Mr. Johnson,

We thank you for your inquiry for our products. In reply, we are enclosing you a quotation sheet and the samples for your test. The other terms are as follows:

Shipment: To be effected within 20 days from receipt of the deposit by T/T.

Packing : One small opp bag/pcs, a big opp bag/dozen, 144 pcs to a standard export box, or as your requirement.

Payment: 30% deposit by T/T and the balance against B/L copy.

Insurance: For 110% invoice value covering All Risks and War Risk as per the relevant Ocean Marine Cargo Clause of the People's Insurance Company of China dated Jan. 1st, 1981.

This offer is subject to your reply here before 18th April our time.

We are looking forward to your order.

Yours Sincerely,

Zhejiang Xinxin Ornament Co., Ltd.

Li Ning

Foreign Sales Department

Enclosure: Quotation Sheet

ZHEJIANG Xinxin Ornament CO., LTD.		
PRODUCT PHOTO	Item No.	FR1001
	Description	Fasion Finger Ring（925 Sterling Silver）
	CIFC3 New York	USD 8/PC
	Country of Origin	China
	Min. Order Qty.	500 PCS
	Shipment	20 days after the deposit
	Packing	small opp bag/pcs (inner)
	Terms of Payment	T/T in advance or L/C at sight

Continue

PRODUCT PHOTO	Item No.	FR1002
	Description	Sterling Silver
	CIFC3 New York	USD10/PC
	Country of Origin	China
	Min. Order Qty.	500 PCS
	Shipment	20 days after the deposit
	Packing	small opp bag/pcs (inner)
	Terms of Payment	T/T in advance or L/C at sight

PRODUCT PHOTO 	Item No.	FR1003
	Description	Sterling Silver
	CIFC3 New York	USD15/PC
	Country of Origin	China
	Min. Order Qty.	500 PCS
	Shipment	20 days after the deposit
	Packing	small opp bag/pcs (inner)
	Terms of Payment	T/T in advance or L/C at sight

PRODUCT PHOTO	Item No.	FR1004
	Description	Sterling Silver
	CIFC3 New York	USD12/PC
	Country of Origin	China
	Min. Order Qty.	500 PCS
	Shipment	20 days after the deposit
	Packing	small opp bag/pcs (inner)
	Terms of Payment	T/T in advance or L/C at sight

Task 2 Contract Signing

 Writing Background

浙江欣欣饰品有限公司外贸部业务员李宁的函电发出后不久，就收到了美国 Sun Trading Co., Ltd. 的邮件及订单。

Dear Mr.Li,

Thank you for your quotation of 31 March and the samples of fashion finger rings. We find both the quality and prices are satisfactory, so we are pleased to place an order with you as follows.

Thank you for your e-mail and PI. We are glad to place Order No. ST1867 as follows:

Order No.	ST1867	Date	April 10, 2013	
Commodity	925 Sterling Silver			
Art No.	FR1001	FR1002	FR1003	FR1004
Packing	1pc/opp bag	1pc/ opp bag	1pc/ opp bag	1pc/ opp bag
Price Term	CIF New York Amount: USD84 960.00			
Unit Price	USD 8/pc	USD 10/pc	USD 15/pc	USD 12/pc
Quantity	1 440 pcs	2 160 pcs	2 880 pcs	720 pcs
Shipment	Not later than May 30, 2013, allowing transshipments			
Payment	30% by T/T as a deposit and the balance against B/L copy			
Insurance	Covered by the seller for 110% invoice value against All Risks and War Risk			

Please send us your sales contract/sales confirmation as soon as possible.

Thanks & Regards,
Smith Johnson

Writing Task

请根据订单 ST1867 的内容，代浙江欣欣饰品有限公司撰写签约函，并起草一份销售合同寄给美国 Sun Trading Co., Ltd.，要求会签后返回一份存档。

Writing Guide

1. 销售合同（Sales Contract/销售确认书）

After a firm offer is accepted or an acceptance is confirmed, a contract or a sales confirmation should be made out generally by the sellers and signed by both parties. A sales contract or a sales confirmation (S/C) will go into effect immediately upon signature.

A contract or a sales confirmation must contain all the particulars agreed upon during the course of negotiation, but the contract contains also such conventional clauses as inspection and claims, arbitration and force majeure, etc.. In case of dispute, this is the only authentic document on which judgment is based.

一份正式的贸易合同通常由三个部分构成：约首（Preamble）、约文（Body）和约尾（Witness Clause）。

约首通常包括合同名称、合同号码、缔约日期、缔约当事人、缔约地点、当事人的合法依据、缔约缘由等。

约文通常包括定义条款、一般条款、基本条款、有效期、终止、让与、不可抗力、适用法律、仲裁、诉讼管辖、通知手续、完整条款、修改等。

约尾通常包括文字效力、份数、见证人、附件、当事人签字、盖章等。

2. 合同内容

贸易合同通常包含以下内容：

① 合同名称及其编号（Title and Reference）；
② 序言/约首（Preamble）；
③ 商品名称（Name of Commodity）；
④ 品质条款（Quality Clause）；
⑤ 数量条款（Quantity Clause）；
⑥ 价格条款（Price Clause）；
⑦ 包装条款（Packing Clause）；
⑧ 交货条款（Delivery Clause）；
⑨ 支付条款（Payment Clause）；
⑩ 保险条款（Insurance Clause）；
⑪ 检验条款（Inspection Clause）；
⑫ 索赔条款（Claim Clause）；
⑬ 仲裁条款（Arbitration Clause）；
⑭ 不可抗力条款（Force Majeure Clause）；
⑮ 违约及解除契约条款（Breach and Cancellation of Contract Clause）；
⑯ 其他条款（Miscellaneous Clause）。

3. 合同的主要条款

1）品质条款（Quality Clause）。商品的品质（Quality of Goods）就是商品的内在素质（包括物理的、化学的、生物的构造、成分和性能）和外表形态的综合。

2）数量条款（Quantity Clause）。商品的数量是指以一定的度量衡单位表示的货物重量、件数、长度、面积、容积等。

3）价格条款（Price Clause）。合同中的价格条款，一般包括商品的单价和总值两项基本内容。对外贸易中商品的价格通常是指单位数量进出口商品的价格，称为单价（Unit Price），是进出口商品价值的货币表现。对外贸易商品的单价一般由四个部分组成：计价货币、单位金额、计量单位和价格术语，如 US $ 100.00 Per M/T FOB SHENZHEN。

4）包装条款（Packing Clause）。包装条款主要规定货物的包装方式、包装材料、包装费用的负担和运输标志等。

5）交货条款（Delivery Clause）。在销售合同中，交货条款一般是指装运条款。合同中的装运条款一般包括装运时间（Time of Shipment）、装运港/地（Port/Place of Loading）、目的港/地（Port/Place of Destination）、货物运输方式（Means of Transport）以及装运的附加条件。

6）支付条款（Payment Clause）。支付条款主要规定用何种付款方式。如信用证付款，则须规定信用证的类别、金额，信用证到达时间，信用证有效期及有效地点等。

7）保险条款（Insurance Clause）。保险条款主要规定由哪方办理保险、投保何种险别、保险金额的确定方法、依照哪些保险条款及该条款的生效日期。

4. 签约函的撰写

In a letter sending or making mention of a contract, the following contents should be included.

1) Express your pleasure for receiving the order.

2) State that you have enclosed a sales contract or a sales confirmation.

3) Request the return of one copy duly signed for your file.

4) Express your expectation of the counter-signature, promise or hope that the contract would be fulfilled smoothly and successfully, and that the mutual business would be expanded in the future.

签约函首先要表达对客户订单的感谢以及自己的高兴之情，然后随函寄上销售合同或销售确认书，以供对方会签，最后预祝双方合作愉快。

Reference E-mail

Dear Mr. Johnson,

We are glad to receive your order No. ST1867 and many thanks.

We are enclosing our signed Sales Confirmation No. ZX13005 in duplicate, please counter sign and return one copy to us for file. If there is any problem or misunderstanding, don't hesitate to call us.

You may rest assured that your order will receive our best attention.

Thanks & Regards,

Li Ning

Enclosure: Reference Sales Contract

SALES CONTRACT

编号 S/C No.: ZX13005

日期 Date: April 20, 2013

签约地点 Signed At :Yiwu, China

卖方 Sellers：ZHEJIANG XINXIN ORNAMENT CO., LTD.
ROOM 1561, XINCHENG MANSION, BINWANG ROAD, YIWU, ZHEJIANG, P.R.CHINA

买方 Buyers：SUN TRADING CO., LTD.
#356 PALAN STREET, NEW YORK, AMERICA

兹买卖双方同意成交下列商品，双方订立条款如下：

The contract is made by and agreed between the buyer and the seller in accodance with the terms and conditions stupilated below:

1. 品名及规格 Name of Commodity and Specification	2. 数量 Quantity	3. 单价及价格条款 Unit Price	4. 金额 Amount USD	5. 总值 Total Value USD
Fasion Finger Ring		CIF Sydney		
FR1001	1 440pcs	USD8/ pc	11 520.00	
FR1002	2 160 pcs	USD10/ pc	21 600.00	84 960.00
FR1003	2 880 pcs	USD15/ pc	43 200.00	
FR1004	720 pcs	USD12/ pc	8 640.00	

数量及总值均可有 10%的增减，由卖方决定。

With 10% more or less both in amount and quantity allowed at the Seller's option.

6. 包装

Packing：One small opp bag/pcs, a big opp bag/dozen, 144 pcs to a standard export box, or as your requirement.

7. 装运期限：☑ 收到定金后 30 天内发货，允许转运。

Time of Shipment: ☑ Within 30 days after receipt of the deposit allowing transshipment.

8. 装运口岸：宁波。

Port of Loading: Ningbo.

9. 目的港：纽约。

Port of Destination: New York.

10. 付款条件：☑ 发货前 30 天付 30%定金，其余凭提单副本付款。

Terms of Payment: ☑ 30% deposit by T/T 30 days before shipment and the balance against B/L copy.

11. 保险：☑ 按中国保险条款，保综合险及战争险（不包括罢工险）。

Insurance: ☑ Covering All Risks and War Risk only (excluding S.R.C.C.) as per the China Insurance Clauses.

12. 装船标记；空白唛头

Shipping Marks: N/M[4].

13. 备注（REMARKS）

卖方 THE SELLERS ZHEJIANG XINXIN ORNAMENT CO., LTD.	买方 THE BUYERS SUN TRADING CO., LTD.

Task 3 Payment

合同签署后不久，公司要求林枫代表李宁去函美国 Sun Trading Co., Ltd.，希望尽快汇

出 30%的定金，以便欣欣公司尽早安排生产，按时发货。邮件发出后 2 天，就收到了美国公司的函电及付款凭证，对方希望欣欣公司在收到款项后即向其通告。

公司去函如下：

Dear Mr. Johnson,

Re: Our Sales Confirmation No. ZX13005

With reference to the 600 dozen fashion finger rings under our S/C No. ZX13005, we wish to draw your attention to the fact that the date of shipment is approaching, but we still have not received your covering deposit. Please remit the deposit as early as possible so that you can receive the goods on time.

We hope to receive your favorable news soon.

Best Regards,

Li Ning

2 天后，美国公司来函如下：

Dear Li,

Today we have made the deposit to you. Attachment is the T/T swift copy, please check it. I think you will receive the money quite soon. Once you receive the money, please let me know.

Best Regards,

Smith Johnson

Writing Task

请以浙江欣欣饰品有限公司业务员李宁的名义写一封邮件，告知美国 Sun Trading Co., Ltd.已收到定金，并正安排生产，承诺 30 天后备齐货物发运。

Writing Guide

国际贸易中货款的结算是每笔业务的关键环节。货款收付涉及买卖双方的信用，使用何种货币，在什么时候、以何种方式支付等问题，这些问题直接关系到双方的切身利益。在进出口交易中，货款结算主要有三种方式：汇付、托收和信用证。其中信用证对双方来说最为安全。

1. 汇付

汇付又称汇款，是付款人通过银行，使用各种结算工具将货款汇交收款人的一种结算方式。汇付属于商业信用，采用顺汇法。按汇款方式的不同，又可分为电汇、信汇和票汇。

汇付的当事人有四个：汇款人、收款人、汇出行、汇入行。

汇付的优点在于手续简便、费用低廉。

汇付的缺点是风险大、资金负担不平衡。因为以汇付方式结算，可以是货到付款，也可以是预付货款。如果是货到付款，卖方向买方提供信用并融通资金；预付货款则买方向卖方提供信用并融通资金。不论是哪一种方式，风险和资金负担都集中在一方。

2. 托收

托收是出口人在货物装运后，开具以进口方为付款人的汇票（随附或不随附货运单据），委托出口地银行通过它在进口地的分行或代理行代出口人收取货款的一种结算方式。托收属于商业信用，采用的是逆汇法，主要有付款交单和承兑交单两种方式。

托收的当事人主要有四个：委托人、托收银行、代收银行、付款人。

托收对出口人的风险较大，承兑交单比付款交单的风险更大。跟单托收方式是出口人先发货，后收取货款，因此对出口人来说风险较大。托收对进口人比较有利，可以免去开证的手续以及预付押金，还可获得预借货物的便利。

3. 信用证

信用证是指开证银行应申请人的要求并按其指示向第三方开立的载有一定金额的、在一定的期限内凭符合规定的单据付款的书面保证文件。信用证是国际贸易中最主要、最常用的支付方式。

买卖双方对每一种结算方式，都应从手续费用、风险和资金负担的角度综合权衡利弊。

Payment is an important issue in international trade. A company cannot keep running well without getting payments for its products or services. No export transaction can be regarded as successful until the money has been paid for the goods delivered overseas, and the proceeds have been safely credited to the exporter's account. Over the years, standard methods of payment used by those engaged in foreign trade have been established. In international trade, there are mainly three payment methods.

1. Remittance

There are three types: Telegraphic Transfer (T/T) [5], Mail Transfer (M/T) [6] and Banker's Demand Draft (D/D) [7].

2. Collection

There are two main types: Documents against Payment (D/P) [8] and Documents against Acceptance (D/A) [9].

3. Letter of Credit (L/C)

L/C is the most generally used method of payment in international trade. It is reliable and safe for both sellers and buyers. There are various types of L/C, such as irrevocable documentary credit, revolving credit, standby credit and back-to-back credit, etc.

The parties of L/C include beneficiary, applicant, opening bank, advising bank, negotiating bank, paying bank and so on.

The procedures of L/C business:

① The buyer and the seller conclude a sales contract providing for payment by documentary credit;

② The buyer instructs his or her bank—the issuing bank to issue a credit in favor of the seller (beneficiary);

③ The issuing bank asks another bank, usually in the country of the seller, to advise and perhaps also to add its confirmation to the documentary credit;

④ The advising or confirming bank informs the seller that the credit has been issued;

⑤ The beneficiary checks the credit and presents the documents to the negotiating bank;

⑥ The negotiating bank sends the documents to the paying bank for reimbursement;

⑦ The applicant pays the money and gets the documents from the paying bank.

The main features of L/C:

① The opening bank is the first payer of L/C;

② L/C is a self-sufficient instrument;

③ L/C business is a pure documentary one.

When a transaction is concluded, the buyer, as a rule, is under obligation to establish a letter of credit with his or her bank within the time stipulated in the sales contract/confirmation. It is usual practice in export trade that the L/C is to be established and to reach the seller one month before the date of shipment so as to give the seller ample time to make preparations for shipment, such as making the goods ready and booking shipping space.

However, there may be circumstances where the buyer fails to establish the letter of credit, or the letter of credit does not reach the seller in time. Then a letter, usually an E-mail has to be sent to the buyer to urge him or her to expedite the L/C. The first message sent should therefore be a polite note saying that the goods ordered are ready but the relevant letter of credit has not yet come to hand. Messages urging establishment of letter of credit must be written with tact. Their aim is to persuade the buyer to cooperate more closely and in fact to fulfill his or her obligations.

Reference E-mail

Dear Johnson,

Today we have received your deposit, so we begin to process the rings. About 30 days later, we shall finish your order and ship the goods to you. Please don't worry about it!

Best Regards,

Li Ning

Task 4 Packing

Writing Background

在合同 ZX13005 履行过程中，美国 Sun Trading Co., Ltd.发来函电要求改进包装。

Dear Mr. Li,

Thank you for your E-mail.

As far as packing is concerned, we hope you can improve it. Would you please pack 144 pcs in a foam plastic bag, then to a carton?

By the way, please stencil the words "KEEP DRY" on the carton. We trust that you will give special care to the packing in order to avoid damage in transit.

Best Regards,

Johnson

Writing Guide

在国际贸易中，除少数散装货和裸装货外，绝大多数商品都需要有适当的包装。商品包装是保护商品在流通过程中品质完好和数量完整的重要条件，也是实现商品使用价值和增加价值的必要手段之一。出口商品的包装，应力求科学、经济、牢固、美观、实用。

商品包装可分为运输包装和销售包装两大类。运输包装又称大包装、外包装，是将货物装入特定容器或以特定方式成件或成箱的包装。运输包装的作用：保护商品在长时间或远距离的运输过程中不被撞坏或散失；方便商品的搬运、储存和运输。销售包装又称小包装、内包装，是在商品制造出来以后，以适当的材料或容器进行初次包装。销售包装除了保护商品的品质外，还能美化和宣传商品，便于陈列展销、吸引顾客，方便消费者的识别、选购、携带和使用。

Packing is very important for the goods. It needs more care in export trade than in domestic trade. It has been estimated that as much as 70% of all cargo loss could be prevented by proper packaging. The real art of packing is to get the contents into a nice, compact shape that will stay that way during the roughest journey. There are two forms of packing: ①large packing/outer packing, packing for transportation; ②small packing/inner packing, packing for sales.

There are many packing containers, such as bag, sack, carton, case, box, crate, drum, bale, can or tin, carboy, bundle, container, pallet and so on.

There are three principal types of marking which may have to be done on export package:

1）The consignee's own distinctive marks—They include the name of port of destination.

2）Any official mark required by authorities—Some countries require the name of the country origin of the goods to be marked on every package, and weight and dimensions may also be required.

3）Special instructions or warnings—Special instructions regarding manner of handling, lifting, loading, etc., and various warnings are to be stenciled on the packages for the benefit of both the owner and the carrier, such as

THIS SIDE UP **TOP**

FRAGILE **KEEP DRY**

USE NO HOOKS **OPEN THIS END**

DO NOT STOW ON DECK　　**LIFT HERE**

GLASS WITH CARE　　**HANDLE WITH CARE**

Reference E-mail

Dear Mr. Johnson,

Your E-mail has been carefully noted.

As to packing, we shall put a gross[10] in a foam polybag and then to a carton. We'll also stencil the words "KEEP DRY" on the carton in accordance with your requirements. Please don't worry about it.

We treasure the chance to cooperate with you very much and we are confident of our capability to do this business.

Best Regards,

Li Ning

Task 5　Sending Shipping Documents

Writing Background

浙江欣欣饰品有限公司业务员李宁写邮件，告知对方：货物已于 2013 年 5 月 25 日发出，要求立即支付余款，公司收款后会马上将整套相关装运单据寄出。

Dear Johnson,

How are you?

We already shipped the goods on May 25, 2013. Now we've just got the B/L, attachments are the B/L copy, insurance policy copy, invoice and packing list. Please check them.

You can ask us freely for any questions. If everything is OK, we'll just wait for you arranging the balance payment for us so that we can send you full original documents at an earlier date.

Best Regards,

Li Ning

Zhejiang Xinxin Ornament Co., Ltd.

美国 Sun Trading Co., Ltd.外商 Johnson 承诺尽快付清余款，并希望浙江欣欣饰品有限公司在收到款项后立即寄出装运单据。

Dear Li,

Thank you for your e-mail.

We will arrange the balance payment soon. When you receive the balance payment, please send us the ready documents immediately, and tell me as soon as you send them.

1）Invoice: three original and one copy;
2）Packing List: three original and one copy;
3）B/L: three original and three copies;
4）Insurance: one original and one copy.

Best Regards,
Johnson
Sun Trading Co., Ltd.

Writing Task

请以浙江欣欣饰品有限公司业务员李宁的名义写一封邮件，表示该公司已收到美国 Sun Trading Co., Ltd.的余款，并寄出了相关单据。

Reference E-mail

Dear Johnson,

Thanks for your balance payment and your support.

We've just received the balance amount from our bank, so we send you the full set of documents now. Please check them. If you have any questions, please do not hesitate to contact us.

By the way, if you have any plans for new business, please let us know at once, and we will try our best to cooperate with you all the time.

Best Regards,
Li Ning

Task 6 Transaction Review

Writing Background

浙江欣欣饰品有限公司与美国 Sun Trading Co., Ltd.刚完成了一笔愉快的交易。美国公司收到货物后，对欣欣公司的时尚戒指非常满意，希望以后多多合作，并要求推荐新款产品。

Writing Task

请以浙江欣欣饰品有限公司外贸部业务员李宁的名义，给美国 Sun Trading Co., Ltd.业务代表 Johnson 发一封电子邮件，说明很高兴得知对方满意自己的产品，希望有机会再次合作，并向其推荐新产品。

Writing Guide

出口商收回货款，进口商满意产品，意味着一笔交易的圆满结束。此时，一封交易回顾函显得尤其重要。它可以帮助进出口双方回顾愉快的合作历程，增进彼此了解，加深彼此之间的感情。交易回顾函可以从以下方面着手撰写：

1）感谢对方的合作使交易得以顺利完成；

2）希望今后有更多的合作机会，并借此推介其他产品等。

When the exporter (or the negotiating bank) presents the whole set of documents to the issuing bank, then the relevant transaction enters the last stage — transaction review. Writing transation review correspondence is one of the most important operation steps for the exporter at this stage. It is mainly the retrospect of the said transaction, which is of great help to establish along-standing business relationship between the Buyer and the Seller. Since the transaction has been carried out quite smoothly, it is not so strict with wording and sentence-making when writing. The transaction review correspondence may contain the following points.

1. Looking back on the positive side of the transaction

1）Appreciating the efforts made by the other party;

2）Showing pleasure for enhancing the understanding between two parties thanks to the transaction.

2. Looking into the future business

1）Expressing the wish for further expanding cooperation;

2）Expecting repeated orders;

3）Hoping for long-term trade relations;

4）Entrusting the customer with agency;

5）Recommending new products.

Reference E-mail

Dear Johnson,

Have you received your fashion rings? Do the rings meet your needs well? Needless to say, with the development of our trade relations, there will be more topics of interest to be discussed between us. We are expecting your advice.

Since you might be aware of the new development in our product range, we are airmailing to you a copy of our latest illustrated price list. If any item interests you, please let us know. We will give you a special discount of 3% for orders exceeding USD100 000 to promote sales at your end.

We hope our handing of your orders will lead to further transaction between us and look forward to your favorable reply.

Best Regards,
Li Ning

Specimen Letters & E-mails

(1)Inquiry 1

Sunshine Trading Co., Ltd.
P.O.Box: 243598, Amman, 11123, Jordan
Tel: 962-6-657852 Fax: 962-6-658943
E-mail: zuy@power.com

September 6, 2008

International Trading Co., Ltd.
No. 598, Zhongshan Road,
Shanghai, China

Dear Zhang,

We are interested to buy large quantities of car speakers and shall appreciate it if you would give us a quotation per pair FOB Shanghai, inclusive of our 3% commission.

We should also be obliged if samples and brochure could be forwarded to us.

We used to purchase this article from Japan but we now prefer to buy from your corporation because we are given to understand that you are able to supply large quantities at more attractive prices. What's more, we have confidence in the quality of Chinese products.

We look forward to hearing from you soon.

Yours Sincerely,

Sunshine Trading Co., Ltd.
Paul Jones
Manager of Purchasing Department

(2) Inquiry 2

Zhejiang Machinery & Equipment Imp. & Exp. Corp.

No. 131, Jiefang Road, Hangzhou, China

Tel: 86-571-87060998 Fax: 86-571-87060997

Feb. 15, 2010

Mr. Smith
Dept. of International Sales
Vermeer Manufacturing Company
P.O. Box 203/3856, New Sharon Road
Pella, Iowa 50319
USA

Dear Mr. Smith,

Re: Parts for Machine Type B-114

We purchased from you ten sets of the captioned machine in 2009. The machine has been very satisfactory.

However, at present we need a large quantity of parts/ accessories as per the enclosed list. Please send us as soon as possible your proforma invoice. You are kindly requested to quote the FOB New York rate.

The parts and accessories are urgently needed, so we wish to receive your proforma invoice at an early date.

Sincerely Yours,
Zhejiang Machinery & Equipment Imp. & Exp. Corp.
Jennifer Wang
Manager

Encl.: a copy of inquiry list

(3) Inquiry 3

Alice Trading Co., Ltd.

P.O.Box: 3267E Asbury Ave #418, Denver, CO 8010,USA

Tel: 001-85657852 Fax: 001-6-86658978

E-mail: stug@alice.com

April 6, 2013

Tian Ting Co., Ltd.
No. 601, Jiefang Road,
Hangzhou, China

Dear Miss Zhou,

We received your brochure today.

We believe that you will do well here in the USA. Kindly send us further details of your prices and terms of sales. We would like you to make every effort to quote a competitive price in order to conclude our business.

We look forward to hearing from you soon.

Sincerely Yours,
Alice Trading Co., Ltd.
Simon Manager

(4) Reply

Zhejiang Jinyi Bicycles Co., Ltd.
No. 321, Qiutao North Street, Jinhua, Zhejiang, China
Tel: 86-579-82273576 Fax: 86-579-82274856
E-mail: jhjane@hotmail.com

December 20, 2009

Star International Trading Est.
Av. R.Vander Bruggen 43
Brussels, Belgium

Dear Mr. Robin,

Thank you for inquiring about our Silver Streak mountain bike.

Unfortunately this model is temporarily out of stock because of the Christmas rush, but we could deliver 1000 units to you by the end of January and give a seasonal discount of 2%.

We also have other models that could be delivered immediately. The Flying 102 model, for instance, is becoming one of our most popular bikes because it is light weight but very strong, although the cost is a little more than the Silver Streak. If you would like to receive Christmas delivery of this or any other bike in the enclosed brochure, please let us know.

In the meantime, we send you our best wishes for a happy holiday season.

Yours Sincerely,

Zhejiang Jinyi Bicycles Co., Ltd.
Jane Ying
Sales Manager

(5) Offer 1

Huxing Import & Export Co., Ltd.
No.356, Nanjing Road, Shanghai, China
Tel: 86-21-28237546 Fax: 86-21-28248765

May 20, 2010

Arc Euro Trade
19 Barkby Lane, Syston
Leicester, Le7 2BA
U.K.

Dear Mr. Smith,

We are pleased to receive your inquiry of May 10 and to hear that you are interested in our HY series, especially HY15, HY18 and HY20.

We would like to quote as follows based on per 20' FCL.

Commodity	Article No.	CIF C5 London per piece	Cartons per 20' FCL
Toys	HY15	USD25.11	1542 CTNS
	HY18	USD16.33	1437 CTNS
	HY20	USD20.88	1400 CTNS

Packing: One piece to a carton.

Shipment: To be made shipment within one month after receipt of the relevant L/C.

Payment: By L/C at sight.

Insurance: For 110% invoice value covering All Risks and War Risk.

We will keep this offer valid only for 7 days.

In addition, we have sent the samples you requested. In order to assist you in promoting sales at the initial stage, they are free of charge.

We are looking forward to your initial order.

Yours Sincerely,
Huxing Imp. & Exp. Co., Ltd.
Jessica Zhang
Manager

(6) Offer 2

Universal Trading Co., Ltd.

Jinxing Building 2-403 , Zhongshan Road, Shanghai, China

Tel: 86-21-23567891 Fax: 86-21-25768932

E-mail: utliming@hotmail.com

August 3, 2009

Discovery Belgium SPRL
Av. R. Vander Bruggen 95
1090 Brussels, Belgium

Dear Ms. Hopkins,

We thank you for your inquiry for our peanuts.

We are making you, subjected to your acceptance reaching us not later than August 10, the following offer:

"20 metric tons of Hand-picked and Ungraded Shandong Peanuts, at CNY 800 per metric ton CIF Antwerp, for shipment during October/November, 2009. Other terms and conditions are the same as usual."

As there is no direct steamer available from here to Antwerp, the products will have to be transshipped at Singapore. Please allow transshipment.

For your information, of late there has been a large demand for peanuts and such a growing demand can only result in increased price. However, you may get profit by this advancing market if you let us have your acceptance immediately.

Yours Faithfully,
Universal Trading Co., Ltd.
Jolin Li
Sales Manager

(7) Offer 3

Sinbao Trading Co., Ltd.

Xin Hua Building 5-506 , Sicun Road, Shanghai, China

Tel: 86-21-33567942 Fax: 86-21-33567941

E-mail: Liming@hotmail.com

February 27, 2013

Albert Foods Co., Ltd
liitonjoentie 50,44930 Peninki
Finland

Dear Mr. Jones,

We thank you for your inquiry for both groundnuts and walnut meat CNF Copenhagen dated

February 21.

In reply, we offer firm, subjected to your reply reaching us on March 26, 250 metric tons of groundnuts, handpicked, shelled and ungraded at CNY2 000 net per metric ton CNF Copenhagen. Shipment is to be made within two months after receipt of your order payment by L/C payable by sight draft.

Please note that we have quoted our most favorable price and are unable to entertain any counter-offer.

As you are aware, there has lately been a larger demand for the above commodities. Therefore, such rising tendency will be likely to result in increased prices. However, we can give you the quoted price if you send us a reply within the time limit.

Sincerely,
Sinbao Trading Co., Ltd.
Li Ming

(8) Offer 4

Jiahua Trading Co., Ltd.

Jinghua Building 8-806 , Yanan Road, Hangzhou, China

Tel: 86-0571-87684351   Fax: 86-0571-87684352

E-mail: Lucy@hotmail.com

April15, 2013

Best Bag Trading Co., Ltd
1267 Beach Blvd, Huntington Beach,
CA, USA

Dear Mr. Jones,

We thank you for your E-mail dated April 8 inquiring about our leather handbags. As requested, we take pleasure in offering you, subjected to our final confirmation, 300 dozen deerskin handbags style No.MS190 at US$ 124.00 per dozen CIF New York. Shipment will be effected within 20 days after receipt of the relevant L/C issued by your first class bank in our favor upon signing Sales Contract.

We are also manufacturing various kinds of leather purses and waist belts for exportation, and hereby enclose a brochure of products for your reference. We hope some of them will meet your tastes and needs.

If we can be of any further help, please feel free to let us know. Customers' inquiries are always met with our careful and prompt attention.

Sincerely,
Jiahua Trading Co., Ltd.
Lucy

(9) Offer 5

Jinglong Co., Ltd.

Huadu Building 1605, Shenyang Road, Qingdao, China

Tel: 86-0532- 87756142 Fax: 86-0532-87756141

E-mail: Lily@hotmail.com

July 23, 2009

Nippon Foods Co., Ltd

Gifu-City Gifu-Pref 300-8385

Japan

Dear Mr. Sam,

Re: SWC Sugar

We are in receipt of your E-mail of July 17, 2009 asking us to offer 10 000 metric tons of the subject sugar for shipment to Japan and appreciate very much your interest in our product.

To comply with your request, we are offering you the following:

1) Commodity: Qingdao Superior White Crystal Sugar;

2) Packing: to be packed in new gunny bag of 100 kgs each;

3) Quantity: ten thousand (10 000) metric tons;

4) Price: USD five hundred and ninety five (US$595.00) per metric ton, FOB Qingdao;

5) Payment: 100% by irrevocable and confirmed letter of credit to be opened in our favor through a bank in Qingdao and to be drawn at sight;

6) Shipment: three or four weeks after the receipt of letter of credit by the first available boat sailing to Yokohama direct.

Please note that we do not have much ready stock on hand. Therefore, it is important that, in order to enable us to effect early shipment, your letter of credit should be opened in time if our price meets with your approval.

We are awaiting your reply.

Sincerely,

Jinglong Co., Ltd.

Lily

(10) Packing 1

Huaxia Trading Co., Ltd.

Huaxia Building 1005, Zhongshan Road, Shanghai, China

Tel: 86-021- 87235467 Fax: 86-021-87235468

E-mail: Jerry@126.com

December 12, 2013

Siggest Kuwait
p.o box -16535,
Farwaniya fire station st,
Farwaniya, kuwait

Dear Tom,

The 12 000 cycles you ordered will have been ready for dispatch by December 16th. Since you require them for onward shipment to Kuwait and Oman, we are arranging for them to be packed in seaworthy containers.

Each bicycle is packed in a corrugated cardboard, and 20 are banned together and wrapped in sheet plastic. A container holds 240 cycles. The whole cargo would therefore comprise 50 containers, each weighing 8 tons. Dispatch can be made from our works by rail to be forwarded from Shanghai harbor. The freight charges from works to Shanghai are US$ 80 per container, totally US$ 4 000 for this consignment, excluding container hire, which will be charged to your account.

Please let us have your delivery instruction.

Yours Faithfully,
Huaxia Trading Co., Ltd.
Jerry Zhuang
Sales Manager

(11) Packing 2

Dear Mr. Zhang,

We returned for your file the counter-signed copy of contract No. DG5081 on September 15.

Please mark the bales with our initials SCC in a diamond, under which come the destination Bremen with order No. 4424 below again.

This is to apply to all orders unless otherwise specified.

Yours Faithfully,
Jones

(12) Packing 3

Dear Mr. Zhao,

Order No.KY/2345 200 Dozen Shirts

We are in receipt of your E-mail of June 12 informing us that the captioned goods have been shipped per S.S. "East Wind" and thank you for your invoice No. N2467 in duplicate.

With regard to the packing for ready-made garments, you say that you have taken up the matter with the competent departments and are of the opinion that packing in cartons will prevent skillful pilferage. Such cartons are well protected against moisture. They are light and convenient to handle, etc.. After discussing the matter with our clients, we find that your comments sound quite reasonable. However, we cannot be sure how things will prove to be until the first lot of goods packed in such cartons arrives.

We hold that if the result of packing in cartons turns out to be the satisfaction of your clients, you may continue using this packing in future. Otherwise, we are afraid that this will considerably affect the development of business between us.

You may rest assured that in our mutual interest we shall do everything possible to give you our full cooperation.

As soon as the goods shipped by S.S. "East Wind" reach us, we shall not fail to communicate with you.

Yours Faithfully,
Jones

(13) Payment 1

Dear Sirs,

We spoke to your representative, Mr. Bergman, at the International Automobile Expo. in Tokyo last week, and he showed us a number of snowmobiles which you produce, and informed us of your terms and conditions.

We were impressed with the vehicles, and have decided to place a trial order for ten of them, your Car No. SM18. The enclosed order, No. 98918, is for prompt delivery as the winter season is only a few weeks away.

As Mr. Bergman assured us that you could meet any order from stock, we have instructed our bank, Bank of China, Tianjin Branch, to open a confirmed letter of credit for USD 108 000 in your favor, valid until December 1, 2009.

Our bank informs us that credit will be confirmed by their agents, Scandinavian Bank, Strindberg Street, Stockholm. You may draw on the agents for the full amount of the invoice at 60 days, and your draft should be presented with the following documents:

Six copies of the bill of lading;

Five copies of the commercial invoice, CIF Tianjin;

Insurance Certificate for USD 118 800 (A. R.);

Certificate of origin;

Certificate of quality.

The credit will cover the invoices, discount and any other bank charges. Please fax us confirming that the order has been accepted and the vehicles can be delivered within the next six weeks.

Yours Faithfully,

Derek Zhang

Purchase Department

(14) Payment 2

Dear Mr. Jones,

With reference to the 4 000 dozen shirts under our Sales Confirmation No.SX260, we wish to draw your attention to the fact that the date of delivery is approaching but up to the present we have not received the covering L/C. Please do your utmost to expedite its establishment so that we may execute the order within the prescribed time.

In order to avoid subsequent amendments, please see to it that the L/C stipulations are in exact accordance with the terms of the contract.

We look forward to receiving your favorable response at an early date.

Sincerely,

Hellen

(15) Shipment 1

Dear Sirs,

We are pleased to inform you that your consignment was shipped yesterday on board S.S. “East Wind” which is sailing directly to Toronto.

A set of the relative shipping document have been sent to you by DHL this morning, thus you may find no trouble in taking the delivery of the goods when they arrive at your end.

We hope this shipment will reach your port in time and turn out to be your entire satisfaction.

Yours Faithfully,

Tom

(16) Shipment 2

Dear Sirs,

We refer to our Purchase Contract No. 758.

Under the terms of the contract, delivery is scheduled for May 2009. We would now like to bring delivery forward to March/April 2009.

We realize that the change of delivery date will be probably inconvenient to you and we offer our sincere apologies. We know that you will understand that we would not ask for earlier delivery if we did not have compelling reasons for doing so.

In view of our longstanding, good commercial relationship, we would be very grateful if you would make a special effort to comply with our request.

We look forward to your early reply.

Yours faithfully,
John

(17) Transaction Review

Dear Amy,

We are pleased to know that the issuing bank has honored our draft against L/C No. 2009CZYK20497N.

You can be sure that the goods shipped will meet your needs just well. We believe the conclusion of this transaction will help to further our mutual understanding and pave the way for more business in the future.

Enclosed is our latest catalogue, in which you may find quite a few new items. If you have any further requirement, please inform us A.S.A.P.

We would like to assure you of our prompt and careful attention in handling your future orders.

Yours Truly,
Aaron Wang

Notes

1. OEM：原始设备商（Original Equipment Manufacturer）的英文缩写。OEM 的基本含义是定牌生产合作，俗称“代工”，即品牌生产者不直接生产产品，而是利用自己掌握的“关键核心技术”负责设计和开发新产品，控制销售和销售“渠道”。品牌拥有者的生产能力有限，甚至连生产线、厂房都没有，为了增加产量和销量、降低上新生产线的风险，乃至为了赢得市场时间，它一般通过合同订购的方式，委托其他同类产品厂家生产，对产品实行低价买断，并直接贴上自己的品牌商标。这种委托他人生产的合作方式即为 OEM，而承接加工任务的制造商就被称为 OEM 厂商，其生产的产品就是 OEM 产品。在 OEM 的情形下，购买方对产品的具体规格基本不参与意见。

2. ODM：原始设计制造商（Original Design Manufacturer）的英文缩写。OEM 的基本特征是技术在外，资本在外，市场在外，只有生产在内；而 ODM 的基本含义是一家厂商根据另一厂商的规格和要求，设计和生产产品。受委托方拥有设计能力和技术水平，基于授权合同生产产品。比较而言，ODM 方式更加注重合作。

3. R&D：R&D（Research and Development）可译为“研究与开发”。

4. N/M：NO MARK 的英文缩写。意指没有唛头，即“空白唛头”，可以在外箱上不显示任何标志。在实际业务中往往是正唛空白，侧唛常规。

5. T/T：电汇（Telegraphic Transfer）的英文缩写，指汇出行应汇款人申请，拍发加押电报/电传或 SWIFT 给在另一个国家的分行或代理行（即汇入行）指示其解付一定金额给收款人的一种汇款方式。

6. M/T：信汇（Mail Transfer）的英文缩写，指汇款人向当地银行交付本国货币，由银行开具付款委托书，用航空邮寄交国外分行或代理行，办理付出外汇业务。采用信汇方式，由于邮程需要的时间比电汇长，银行有机会利用这笔资金，所以信汇汇率低于电汇汇率，其差额相当于邮程利息。

7. D/D：票汇（Demand Draft, Remittance by Banker's Demand Draft），指汇出行应汇款人的申请，代汇款人开立以其分行或代理行为解付行的银行即期汇票（Banker's Demand Draft），支付一定金额给收款人的一种汇款方式。银行在受理票汇业务时，需签发一张汇票给汇款人，并向汇入行寄送汇票通知书。当收款人持汇票向汇入行提取款项时，汇入行在审验汇票和票根无误后，解付票款给收款人。除此之外，票汇的其他手续与电汇、信汇基本相同。

8. Documents against Payment（D/P）：付款交单，出口商的交单以进口商的付款为条件。出口商将汇票连同货运单据交给银行托收时，指示银行只有在进口商付清货款时才能交出货运单据，如果进口商拒付，就拿不到单据提货；进口商付清货款后，银行才把装运单据交给进口商。

9. Documents against Acceptance（D/A）：承兑交单，指出口商的交单以进口商在汇票上承兑为条件。出口商在装运货物后开具远期汇票，连同商业单据通过银行向进口商提示，进口商承兑汇票后，代收银行即将商业单据交给进口商，在汇票到期时，方履行付款义务。由于进口商只要在汇票上办理承兑，即可取得商业单据并凭此提取货物，因而承兑交单方式只适用于远期汇票的托收。承兑交单是国际贸易常用的一种付款方法。出口商通过托收银行指示代收银行在进口商承兑汇票后，向进口商发放所有权及其他货运文件，但出口商将面临进口商不如期结汇之风险。

10. Gross: 数量单位“罗”。1 罗指 12 打，144 件。

Important Words and Phrases

1. in reply（to one's inquiry）	答复某人询盘
2. It would be appreciated…	如果……我们将不胜感激
3. latest	最近的，最新的
e.g. latest catalogue	最新的产品目录
latest price list	最新的报价单
4. leading	主要的
e.g. leading importer	主要进口商
leading market	主要市场
5. look forward to	希望，盼望（后接动名词或名词）
6. place an order with…	向……订购
7. popularity	盛名
e.g. enjoy/win popularity	享有盛名

8. to be firm for…days	有效期为……天
9. to make（send）inquiry for	询购
10. to offer as follows	报盘如下
11. to quote sb. a price for sth.	向某人报某货物价
12. to quote for sth. at…	报某货物价
13. price including commission	含佣价
14. discount / allowance	折扣
15. to take/have/feel be interest in	对……感兴趣
16. to thank sb. for one's inquiry for…	谢谢某人对……的询价
17. You can rest assured of that…	你对……可以放心
18. find a market	销售
19. selling line	销路
20. trial sale/test sale/test market	试销
21. salable goods	畅销货
22. the best selling line (the best seller)	热门货
23. good market	畅销
24. poor(no) market	滞销
25. check /check up / check up on	查对，核对
check with	与……相符
check in	登记，报到；托运，寄存
check out	付账后离开；检验；被认为无误、合格
26. figure	数字；计算
e.g. double figures	两位数
amount in figure	小写金额
in round figures	以整数表示；大概，总而言之；计算，估计，考虑
figure out at	总计，合计
27. means	手段，方式，工具
e.g. by all means	尽一切办法，务必，一定，当然可以
by means of	借助，依靠
28. partial shipment	分批装运
29. shipping documents	装船单据
30. within the stipulated time	在规定的时间内
31. port of shipment	装运港
32. port of discharge	卸货港
33. time of delivery	交货时间
34. voyage charter	定程租船
35. time of shipment	装运期限

36. time charter 定期租船
37. at one's disposal 由某人使用（支配、处理等）
38. carton 纸箱
39. crate 板条箱
40. fiber board case 纤维板箱
41. fit for ocean transportation 适合海洋运输
42. handle with care 小心轻放
43. in a moldy condition 受潮状态
44. jute bag 麻袋
45. kraft paper bag 牛皮纸袋
46. match the sample 与样品相符
47. on (upon) (the)condition that 在……条件下，如果……
48. regarding/ as regards/ in（with）regard to 关于
49. shipping mark 装运标志/唛头
50. freight forwarder 货运代理

Useful Expressions

1. We send you under separate cover a catalogue on the various kinds of cars now available for export.

2. We are interested in buying large quantities of car speakers and shall appreciate it if you would give us a quotation per pair FOB Shanghai, inclusive of our 3% commission.

3. Will you please send us a copy of your catalogue for gloves, with details of your prices and terms of payment?

4. We should also be obliged if samples and brochure could be forwarded to us.

5. As you asked, we are happy to enclose our latest illustrated catalogue and price list.

6. We are separately sending you some samples and feel confident that when you have examined them you will agree that the products are both excellent in quality and reasonable in price.

7. On regular purchases in quantities of not less than 100 dozen of individual items you can obtain a discount of 2%.

8. Payment is to be made by irrevocable L/C at sight.

9. Please feel free to contact us again if you have any further questions on this or any other matters.

10. We will keep this offer valid only for 7 days.

11. This offer is subject to your reply here before 18th September our time.

12. We believe the attractive design and reasonable price must have strong appeal to your customers.

13. We offer the goods on the basis of CIF.

14. Please quote us your favorable price for the articles named.

15. We would like to have your catalogues and price list for study.

16. All the prices quoted are on FOB basis without commission.

17. We are working on your quotation and will contact you soon.

18. In case of need, we can offer you some other products.

19. Please let us know your further requirements.

20. We will work out the offer next day.

21. I will study it with my colleagues and give you a definit reply within three days .

22. We are potential buyers of textile.

23.There is a good demand for cotton textiles in our market. Could you give me a copy of your catalogue?

24. I wonder if your factory produces toys.

25. We think our silks are beautiful and sure there will be a good market for them in your country.

26.We usually order after having seen samples. Please send us some samples.

27. If you can supply the goods as required, please give us a best price.

28. Please consider that we may place an orders for large quantities.

29. We quote you the prices on FOB basis and ensure our prices are the lowest.

30.We have the goods in stock and can ship on receipt of your order.

31. We may place an order for 5000 cases with you immediately.

32. We have received your offer for peanuts, but find your price too high.

33. Please open the covering L/C in our favor according to the terms contracted.

34. We cannot proceed without settling first the terms of payment.

35. Enclosed please find our Sales Contract No. HN456 in duplicate. If you find everything in order, please sign and return one copy for our file.

36. We are pleased to receive your Order No. 123, and you may rest assured that we shall effect shipment strictly as contracted.

37. The shipping documents will be handed to you by Midland Bank of your city against your accepting our 3 months' draft for ￡2500.

38. In compliance with your request, we exceptionally accept delivery against D/P at sight, but this should not be regarded as a precedent.

39. We wish to advice you that the goods under S/C NO. 567 went forward on the steamer "Yunnan" on July 5. They are to be transshipped at Copenhagen and are expected to reach your port in early September.

40. We take this opportunity to inform you that we have shipped the above goods on board S.S. "Taishan", which sails for your port tomorrow. Enclosed please find one set of shipping documents covering this consignment.

41. The shipment of chemical fertilizer under Contract No.7854 will be effected by S.S.

"Eastwind", which is scheduled to leave here on 16th May. Please arrange insurance for this cargo.

42. For the goods under S/C No. 9080, we have booked space on S.S. "Eastwind" due to arrive in London around 19th May. Please communicate with Lambert Bros. Co., London, our shipping agent, for loading arrangements.

43. We do not object to packing in cartons provided the flaps are glued down and the cartons secured by metal bands.

44. If cartons are used, please supply each chemical in strong polythene bags to ensure protection from damp.

45. Cases must have an inner lining of stout, damp-resisting paper.

46. Packing in sturdy wooden cases is essential. Cases must be nailed, battened and secured by overall metal strapping.

47. When packing, please take into account that the boxes are likely to receive rough handling at this end and must be able to withstand transport over very bad roads.

48. We give you on the attached sheet full details regarding packing and marking. These must be strictly observed.

49. The greatest care must be given to packing as any damage in transit would cause us heavy losses.

50. Please use normal export containers unless you receive special instructions from our agents.

51. As the goods will probably be subjected to a through customs examination, the cases should be of a type which can be easily made fast again after opening.

Exercises

1. Write a business letter in indented style and block style according to the information given.

1) Sender's name: Mainrich International Co., Ltd.

2) Sender's address: P.O. Box 3106, Pangham Road, Vientiane.

3) Date: August 16, 2009.

4) Recipient's name: Forward Medical Equipment Co., Ltd.

5) Recipient's address: 88 Zhongshan Road, Kunshan, Jiangsu, China.

6) Salutation: Dear Sirs.

7) Message: We have received your quotation, but the prices are too high. Could you give us a 10% discount?

8) Complimentary close: Yours Faithfully.

9) Signature: Manager Helen.

2. Situation: You are the sales manager of ABC Imp. & Exp. Corp.. Last week, you exhibited your products (rulers) at a trade fair. And now you receive an inquiry from Mr. Smith whom you have talked with at your booth. Please make a reply to the inquiry.

Dear Sirs,

It was a pleasure to visit your booth last week to discuss your measure tool range and the possibility of selling select products into the Singapore and Australia wholesale market.

Continuing our discussion, I would like to inquire cost, package quantity and trading terms for the following interested products as listed below. I will also need to acquire your preferred mode of transaction to arrange samples of selected product, which can be sent directly to my Singapore office or more economically, sent to our Guangzhou office (see the address below).

We look forward to receiving your earliest advice and continuing discussion towards future business.

Interested products: HS02-B, HS12-B, HS03C-12, HS13-C1.

Regards,

Smith

Notes: Prices: on FOB basis, HS02-B: USD 0.8/pc; HS12-B: USD 2/pc; HS03C-12: USD 2.6/pc; HS13-C1: USD 1.5/pc.

3. Please make a quotation sheet according to the following enquiry.

Enquiry

Dear Sirs,

We inform you that one of our clients is in the marked for pencils. It will be highly appreciated if you could quote us your lowest prices, with indication of date of shipment.

We would like to stress the point that the pencils inquired for are made in China, and packed in color boxes of 12pc each. Meanwhile, the goods should be surveyed by a certified public surveyor as to their quality.

In order to facilitate our mutual business, we hope you would send us your quotation sheet for 20,000 boxes of the pencils with prices on FOB basis, so that we could get our client's confirmation.

Your prompt reply would be appreciated.

Sincerely Yours,

John

4. Following is an order, please draft a contract as to the order.

Order No.	ST476		Date	Oct. 9, 2013
Commodity	Cup			
Art No.	TS2356	TS2357	TS2358	TS2359
Packing	1pc/ box	1pc/ box	1pc/ box	1pc/ box
Quantity	6000 pcs	5000 pcs	8000 pcs	6000 pcs
Unit Price	USD1/pc	USD1.5/pc	USD1.8/pc	USD1.5/pc
Price Term	CIF London			
Shipment	Not later than November 30, 2013, allowing partial shipment and transhipments			

续表

Payment	30 days L/C
Insurance	Covered by the seller for 110% invoice value against All Risks and War Risk

5. 请代表买方发邮件给供货方，提出包装要求：货物用内衬防潮纸的瓦楞纸箱包装，并在外箱上刷上菱形标志，在菱形内刷上买方公司的名称缩写字母。

6. 根据以下情景提示，练习对话。

A：你方怎样包装这一批玩具？

B：我们用纸箱。我们希望包装能更吸引人。我们相信我们的设计和颜色符合欧洲人的品味。很感谢你对改进包装所提的建议。

A：吸引人的包装确实能促进销售。那外包装怎样？

B：我们将货物 10 打装 1 个纸箱，毛重 25 公斤。

A：恐怕纸箱不适合海运吧？

B：纸板箱是适合海运的，而且我们用金属条进行了加固。

A：能用木箱代替吗？

B：如果你方坚持，我们可以答应，但是额外的包装费用由你方承担。

7. Write an E-mail to your customer, acknowledging receipt of his order, but regret being unable to accept it on the basis of D/P, and suggest that he should open an L/C.

1.2 Power Tools Export Transaction

Business Background:

浙江考美斯电器有限公司外贸业务员在广交会上认识了来自澳大利亚 Auto Power Co., Ltd.的 Kathy Harbor 女士。在得知他们有求购电动工具的意向后，给对方发去了要求建立业务关系的邮件。对方对其中的五款电动工具有兴趣，要求报盘。经过几番讨价还价，最终达成交易，成功出口产品，收回货款。

Business Requirements:

1. 熟悉公司情况和电动工具产品信息，尤其是角向磨光机。
2. 了解开拓新客户的主要途径，作出合理的选择。
3. 能够运用函电与新客户进行沟通、交流。
4. 熟悉合同条款，会起草销售合同。
5. 能够根据要求审核信用证，并撰写改证函。

Teaching Objective:

培养学生运用函电与客户进行有效沟通，独立开展外贸业务的能力。

Company Profile

Calmex Electrical Appliance Co., Ltd. is located in Yongkang City. It has established itself as a market leader in the power tools industry offering excellent quality, as well as friendly and personal service to the customers ranging from professional users, DIY (do it yourself) and hobby enthusiasts.

Currently, Calmex runs its main business on OEM or ODM basis for independent brands. With the capability of product design, manufacturing and supply market support, Calmex defines itself as the preferred partner of other world-famous power tools brands.

Now Calmex has more than 400 staff, among them around 70 are engineers. The annual output quantity reaches 1.2 million pieces. The strongest items that Calmex produces are metal-working tools, wood-working tools, car-care related tools, stone/concrete-working tools, including Angle Grinders, Car Polishers, Random Orbit Sanders, Cut-off Machines etc., which are our best-sellers both home and abroad.

Calmex has been up to ISO9001[1] international standard in its operations and successfully updated it to Version 2001. It has also applied for international safety approval for most of its products, covering UL[2], CE[3], EMC[4], CSA[5], GS[6], CB[7], NOM[8], SAA[9], and domestic CCC[10], etc..

Through its product innovation, price strategy and commitment to better services, Calmex is now seeking for sustainable development.

Task 1 Establishing Business Relations

Writing Background

浙江考美斯电器有限公司的电动工具出口到欧美许多国家，但澳大利亚市场一直没有被开拓，公司希望外贸业务员在新的一年里有所突破。浙江考美斯电器有限公司的外贸业务员根据公司的现状，对开拓客户的途径进行了认真的思考，并分析了不同途径的优缺点，最后确定以广交会作为开拓客户的最佳选择。

浙江考美斯电器有限公司外贸业务员在参加广交会时认识了来自澳大利亚 Auto Power Co., Ltd.的 Kathy Harbor 女士，得知其公司对一些型号的电动工具比较感兴趣。Auto Power Co., Ltd.的联系方式如下：

Mrs. Kathy Harbor
Purchasing Division
Auto Power Co., Ltd.
19/21 Herdsman Avenue, Sydney, NSW, Australia
Tel: (618) 9732 8458
Fax: (618) 9732 8746
E-mail: harbors@autopower.com

Writing Task

请根据上述背景资料，以考美斯公司外贸部业务员的名义，给 Auto Power Co., Ltd.去函，对本公司情况作简单介绍，同时告之公司网站，以便对方浏览。

Writing Guide

1. Channels to Hunt Prospects

If a firm wishes to open up a market to sell something to or buy something from firms in foreign countries, the person in charge must find out whom he is going to deal with. No customer, no business. Usually, such information is obtainable through the following channels:

① Trade Fairs;
② Internet;
③ Banks;
④ Chambers of Commerce in Foreign Countries;
⑤ Trade Directory;
⑥ Chinese Commercial Counselor's Office in Foreign Countries;
⑦ Business Houses of the Same Trade;
⑧ Advertisements;
⑨ Embassy or Consulate;
⑩ Other Channels.

2. Writing Skills of Business Letters or E-mails on Establishing Business

没有客户就没有业务。在通过上述途径获得客户信息之后，作为贸易的一方应通过函电与之建立业务关系。建立业务关系的函电通常应包括以下内容：介绍获得对方信息的途径；说明去函意图；介绍本公司及产品；告之本公司网站；表达合作愿望等。作为出口商还可附寄产品目录、价格单等材料，作为进口商则可要求对方附寄相关材料。

Having obtained the desired names and addresses of the firms from any of the above sources, the buyer or the seller may start sending e-mails or business letters to the parties concerned. Generally speaking, this kind of e-mail begins by telling the reader how you obtain his/her name and address, expressing your wish of establishing business relations. Then introduce your company, products, business scope, etc..

Reference E-mail

Dear Mrs. Harbor,

Nice to have met you at Canton Fair.

We feel sorry for late contacting with you, since we have been a little bit busy these days.

Taking this opportunity, we would like also to introduce ourselves as one of the specialized power tools manufacturer with 20 years' production experience. And we can say that we are very professional in angle grinder manufacturing.

We mainly offer semi-professional and professional tools, which shares 70% of our total output. We also offer good DIY tools as well, which accounts for 30% of total output. However, the percentage is getting less and less, as most of our customers are improving their quality requirements.

Currently, our biggest OEM customer is ROCY for North America, Australia and Europe. Their order shares about 50% of our total output. We are also the biggest supplier of angle-grinder-similar products, such as car polishers, random orbit sanders and so on. For more details, pls. kindly refer to our website: http://www.calmex.com/ .

If there are some items drawing your attention, pls. feel free to contact us, and we will respond to that ASAP.

Have a nice day!

Best Regards,
Zhejiang Calmex Electrical Appliance Co., Ltd.
Julia Wang
International Sales Department

Task 2 Inquiry and Offer

Writing Background

浙江考美斯电器有限公司外贸部业务员王英（Julia Wang）的函电发出后不久，就收到了澳大利亚 Auto Power Co., Ltd. 的下列询盘：

Dear Miss Wang,

Thanks for your info.

I've now had a chance to go through your products, and I've listed below the models that are of interest:

MS8230, MS8812, MS8804, MS8803.

Can you send me your best prices? How about MOQ? By the way, I'd like to get some samples for testing. Can these be supplied in your usual color of Red/Black? (That would be our standard color as well.)

Looking forward to hearing from you.

Thanks & Regards,
Auto Power Co., Ltd.
Kathy Harbor
Purchasing Division

Writing Task

请以浙江考美斯电器有限公司外贸部业务员的名义对澳大利亚 Auto Power Co., Ltd.的上述询盘进行回复。

Reference E-mail

Dear Kathy,

Thanks for your inquiry for our products.

Pls. refer to the quotation details as follows:

Angle Grinders

Art No. MS8230: USD23.50/PC CIF Sydney

Art No. MS8812: USD15.00/PC CIF Sydney

Art No. MS8804: USD20.40/PC CIF Sydney

Art No. MS8803: USD23.20/PC CIF Sydney

Pls. note the prices we have quoted above are based on our MOQ 500PCS for each item. If you have any questions, pls. feel free to contact me.

And we can make the samples as Red/Black. However, for the first time, I am afraid we have to charge the sample fees from you. Pls. confirm by return, and I will send you the sample PI.

Thanks and Best Regards,

Julia Wang

Task 3 Counter-offer

Writing Background

浙江考美斯电器有限公司给澳大利亚 Auto Power Co., Ltd. 发去报盘邮件，并寄去了所需产品的样品，不久后收到了对方的还盘。

Dear Julia,

Can you please advise REDUCED price for the item on this order? You and I are quite aware of the fact that the cost of raw materials have fallen. Then the price for the item should also be cut down accordingly. Therefore, we can offer our customers more favorable prices, which will in turn make your products more competitive in the international market. Please also note that last time when the cost of raw materials were at the highest level, we agreed upon a new reduced price for this item. So I would expect to see much bigger reduction in price just as that we are getting from other suppliers.

I look forward to your positive reply.

Thanks and Best Regards,
Kathy

Writing task

根据上述客户的还盘内容，以浙江考美斯电器有限公司外贸部业务员的身份，给澳大利亚 Auto Power Co., Ltd.回复邮件，说明之前已经有过一次大幅降价，这次的报价是最低价格，决定维持原价。

Writing Guide

还盘是指受盘人对发盘条件不能完全同意而对原发盘提出修改或变更意愿。还盘相当于一项新的发盘，还盘一旦作出，原发盘即告失效。还盘是对交易条件的实质性变更，有时需要经过多次还盘才能对各项交易条件达成一致，最终成交；有时虽经多次还盘，但因分歧较大而无法成交；有时交易双方无需还盘即可成交。

当受盘人拒绝一项发盘时，应首先感谢对方的发盘，然后说明不能接受的原因，并表示抱歉。如果情况允许，可作还盘，否则可建议以后合作。

A counter-offer is made when an offeree doesn't agree to the terms and conditions of the offer completely and he or she wishes to amend the offer. The offeree may show disagreement to the price, or terms of payment, or terms of shipment, or packing and state his or her own terms instead. Thus a counter-offer is a partial rejection of the original offer and also a counter proposal initiated by the offeree. When a buyer rejects an offer, he or she should write and thank the seller for his or her trouble and explain the reason for rejection. Not to do so would show a lack of courtesy.

The letter of rejection should cover the following points:

1）Thank the seller for his or her offer;

2）Express regret at inability to accept;

3）Make a counter-offer if, in the circumstances, it is appropriate;

4）Suggest other opportunities to do business together.

An acceptance is a statement made by the offeree indicating assent to an offer. When an offeree accepts an offer, he or she should write and thank the offerer. The letter of acceptance should cover the following points:

1）Thank the offerer for his or her offer;

2）Express assent to the offer;

3）Place an order and / or require signing Sales Contract (Confirmation).

Reference E-mail

Dear Kathy,

Thanks for your new e-mail. As for the price issue, you can check price details below. In the list of June 26th, 2009, we have already adjusted the unit price with 7%~10% down, which has resulted from the increased rate of VAT tax rebate and the reduction of the raw material cost as well. Pls. check and comment by return. Thanks!

Waiting for your reply.

Best Regards,
Julia

澳大利亚 Auto Power Co., Ltd.给浙江考美斯电器有限公司回复邮件，表示愿意接受所报价格，并要求寄送形式发票（PI）。

Dear Julia,

Thank you for your last e-mail. Although we think your prices seem to be on the high side, in consideration of the future cooperation between us, we hope to inform you that your latest quotation has been accepted and please send us your PI.

Thanks and Best Regards,
Kathy

收到澳大利亚 Auto Power Co., Ltd. 发来的接受函后，浙江考美斯电器有限公司外贸部业务员王英立即回复邮件，感谢对方的合作，并随附一份形式发票（PI）。

Reference E-mail

Dear Kathy,

Thanks for your cooperation. We succeeded in putting the deal through. Pls. refer to the PI, and confirm it ASAP.

Thanks and Best Regards,
Julia

Enclosure: PI 2009SDT009

Enclosure:

浙江考美斯电器有限公司

ZHEJIANG CALMEX ELECTRICAL APPLIANCE CO., LTD.
ROOM 2501, JIAFA MANSION, JIEFANG WEST ROAD, YONGKANG 321300,
P.R.CHINA
TEL: 86-579-8715004, 86-579-8715619 FAX: 86-579-8791619

PROFORMA INVOICE

To: AUTO POWER CO., LTD.
19/21 HERDSMAN AVENUE, SYDNEY, NSW,
AUSTRALIA

Invoice No.: 2009SDT009
Invoice Date: July 12, 2009
S/C No.:
S/C Date:

From: SHANGHAI **To:** SYDNEY

Letter of Credit No.: **Date:**

Marks and Numbers	Number and Kind of Package (Description of goods)	Quantity	Unit Price	Amount
	2787 CARTONS	2887 SETS	CIF SYDNEY	USD12 737.00
	Angle Grinder			USD15 000.00
	MS8230	542pcs	USD23.50/pc	USD16 320.00
	MS8812	1 000pcs	USD15.00/pc	USD12 644.00
N/M	MS8804	800pcs	USD20.40/pc	
	MS8803	545pcs	USD23.20/pc	

TOTAL: 2 887 pcs USD 56 701.00

TOTAL: SAY UNITED STATES DOLLARS FIFTY SIX THOUSAND SEVEN HUNDRED AND ONE ONLY.

Task 4 Signing Contract

Writing Background

收到上述 PI 后，澳大利亚 Auto Power Co., Ltd.发来如下订货函：

Study Situation 1

Dear Julia,

Thank you for your e-mail and PI. We are glad to place Order No. 264137 as follows:

Commodity	Angle Grinder	Angle Grinder	Angle Grinder	Angle Grinder
Art No.	MS8230	MS8812	MS8804	MS8803
Packing	1pc/carton	1pc/carton	1pc/carton	1pc/carton
Price Term	CIF Sydney Amount: USD56 701.00			
Unit Price	USD23.50/pc	USD15.00/pc	USD20.40/pc	USD23.20/pc
Quantity	542pcs	1 000 pcs	800 pcs	545 pcs
Shipment	Not later than August 30, 2009, allowing partial shipments			
Payment	By L/C at sight			
Insurance	Covered by the seller for 110% invoice value against All Risks and War Risk			

Please send us your sales confirmation in duplicate for counter-signature.

We expect to find a good market for the above goods and hope to place further and larger orders with you in the near future.

Thanks & Regards,

Kathy

Writing Task

请根据以上订单内容，代浙江考美斯电器有限公司起草一份销售合同寄给澳大利亚Auto Power Co., Ltd.，要求会签后返回一份存档。

Reference Sales Contract

SALES CONTRACT

合同号 Contract No.: 2009KMS009

日期 Date: JULY 22, 2009

签约地点 Signed At：JIN HUA, ZHE JIANG

卖方 Sellers：ZHEJIANG CALMEX ELECTRICAL APPLIANCE CO., LTD.

地址 Address：ROOM 2501, JIAFA MANSION, JIEFANG WEST ROAD, YONGKANG 321300, P.R.CHINA

买方 Buyers：AUTO POWER CO., LTD.

地址 Address：19/21 HERDSMAN AVENUE, SYDNEY, NSW, AUSTRALIA

兹买卖双方同意成交下列商品，双方订立条款如下：

The undersigned Sellers and Buyers have agreed to close the following transactions according to the terms and conditions stipulated below:

1. 货物名称及规格 Name of Commodity and Specification	2. 数量 Quantity	3. 单价 Unit Price	4. 金额 Amount USD	5. 总值 Total Value USD
Angle Grinder		CIF Sydney		
MS8230	542 pcs	USD23.50/ pc	12 737.00	56 701.00
MS8812	1 000 pcs	USD15.00/ pc	15 000.00	
MS8804	800 pcs	USD20.40/ pc	16 320.00	
MS8803	545 pcs	USD23.20/ pc	12 644.00	

数量及总值均可有 10%的增减，由卖方决定。

With 10% more or less both in amount and quantity allowed at the Seller's option.

6. 包装每箱一件。

Packing：1pc to a carton.

7. 装运期限：☑ 收到可以转船及分批装运之信用证后 30 天内装出。

Time of Shipment: ☑ Within 30 days after receipt of L/C allowing transshipment and partial shipment.

8. 装运口岸：上海。

Port of Loading: Shanghai.

9. 目的港：悉尼。

Port of Destination: Sydney.

10. 付款条件：☑ 开给我方 100%不可撤销即期付款及可转让可分割之信用证，并须注明可在上述装运日期后 15 天内在中国议付有效。

Terms of Payment: ☑ By 100% confirmed, irrevocable, transferable and divisible Letter of Credit to be available by sight draft and to remain valid for negotiation in China until the 15th day after the aforesaid Time of Shipment.

11. 保险：☑ 按中国保险条款，保综合险及战争险（不包括罢工险）。

Insurance: ☑ Covering All Risks and War Risk only (excluding S.R.C.C.) as per the China Insurance Clauses.

12. 装船标记 Shipping Marks: N/M.

13. 双方同意以装运港中国进出口商品检验局签发的品质和数量（重量）检验证书作为信用证项下议付所提交单据的一部分。买方有权对货物的品质和数量（重量）进行复验，复验费由买方负担。如发现品质和/或数量（重量）与合同不符，买方有权向卖方索赔，但须提供经卖方同意的公证机构出具之检验报告。

It is mutually agreed that the Inspection Certificate of Quality (Weight) issued by China Import and Export Commodity Inspection Bureau at the port of shipment shall be part of the documents to be presented for negotiation under the relevant L/C. The Buyers shall have the right to re-inspect the Quality and Quantity (Weight) of the cargo. The re-inspection fee shall be borne by the Buyers. Should the Quality and/or Quantity (Weight) be found not in conformity with that of the contract, the Buyers are entitled to lodge with the Sellers a claim which should be supported by survey reports issued by a recognized Surveyor approved by the Sellers.

14. 备注（REMARKS）

1）买方须于 2009 年 8 月 1 日前开出本批交易的信用证（或通知卖方进口许可证号码），否则，卖方有权不经通知取消本合同，或不接受买方对本约未执行的全部或一部，或对因此遭受的损失提出索赔。

The Buyers shall have the covering Letter of Credit reached the Sellers (or notify the Import License Number) before August 1st, 2009, otherwise the Sellers reserve the right to rescind without further notice or to accept whole or any part of this Sales Contract not fulfilled by the Buyers, or to lodge a claim for losses this sustained of any.

2）凡以 CIF 条件成交的业务，保额为发票的 110%，投保险别以本销售合同中所开列的为限，买方要求增加保额或保险范围，应于装船前经卖方同意，因此而增加的保险费由买方负责。

For transactions concluded on CIF basis it is understood that the insurance amount will be for 110% of the invoice value against the risks specified in the Sales Contract. If additional insurance amount of coverage is required, the Buyers must have the consent of the Sellers before Shipment and the additional premium is to be borne by the Buyers.

3）品质/数量异议：如买方提出索赔，凡属品质异议须于货到目的口岸之日起 3 个月内提出，凡属数量异议须于货到目的口岸之日起 15 日内提出，对所装运物所提任何异议属于保险公司、轮船公司及其他有关运输机构或邮递机构所负责者，卖方不负任何责任。

QUALITY/QUANTITY DISCREPANCY: In case of quality discrepancy, claim should be filed by the Buyers within 3 months after the arrival of the goods at port of destination; while of quantity discrepancy, claim should be filed by the Buyers within 15 days after the arrival of the goods at port of destination. It is understood that the Sellers shall not be liable for any discrepancy of the goods shipped due to causes for which the Insurance Company, Shipping Company, other transport organizations or post services are liable.

4）本合同所述全部或部分商品，如因人力不可抗拒的原因，以致不能履约或延迟交货，卖方概不负责。

The Sellers shall not be held liable for failure or delay in delivery of the entire lot or a portion of the goods under this Sales Contract on consequence of any Force Majeure incidents.

5）买方开给卖方的信用证上请填注本合同号码。

The Buyers are requested always to quote THE NUMBER OF THIS SALES CONTRACT in the Letter of Credit to be opened in favor of the Sellers.

6）仲裁：凡因执行本合同或与本合同有关事项所发生的一切争执，应由双方通过友好的方式协商解决。如果不能取得协议，则在被告国家根据被告仲裁机构的仲裁程序规则进行仲裁。仲裁决定是终局的，对双方具有同等约束力。仲裁费用除非仲裁机构另有规定，均由败诉一方负担。

Arbitration: All disputes in connection with this Contract or the execution thereof shall be settled by negotiation between two parties. If no settlement can be reached, the case in dispute shall then be submitted for arbitration in the country of defendant in accordance with the arbitration regulations of the arbitration organization of the defendant country. The decision made by the arbitration organization shall be taken as final and binding upon both parties. The arbitration expenses shall be borne by the losing party unless otherwise awarded by the arbitration organization.

7）买方收到本销售合同后立即签回一份；如买方对本合同有异议，应于收到后 5 天内提出，否则认为买方已同意本合同所规定的各项条款。

The Buyers are requested to sign and return one copy of this Sales Contract immediately after receipt of them. Objection, if any, should be raised by the Buyers within five days after the receipt of this Sales Contract, in the absence of which it is understood that the Buyers have accepted the terms and conditions of the Sales Contract.

卖方	买方
THE SELLERS	THE BUYERS
ZHEJIANG CALMEX ELECTRICAL APPLIANCE CO., LTD.	AUTO POWER CO., LTD.

Task 5 Check and Amendment of L/C

Writing Background

合同签署后不久，浙江考美斯电器有限公司收到澳大利亚 Auto Power Co., Ltd 通过银行开来的信用证。信用证全文如下：

ISSUING BANK：AUSTRALIA BANK LTD., SYDNEY

CREDIT NUMBER：SYN88095

DATE OF ISSUE：2009.08.01

EXPIRYDATE AND PLACE: DATE 2009.09.30 PLACE CHINA

APPLICANT：

AUTO POWER CO., LTD.

19/21 HERDSMAN AVENUE,

SYDNEY, NSW, AUSTRALIA

BENEFICIARY：

ZHEJIANG CALMEX ELECTRICAL APPLIANCE CO., LTD.

ROOM 2501, JIAFA MANSION, JIEFANG WEST ROAD

YONGKANG 321300, P.R.CHINA

AMOUNT：USD56 701.00（SAY U.S.DOLLARS FIFTY SIX THOUSAND SENVEN HUNDREDAND ONE ONLY）

THE CREDIT IS AVAILABLE WITH ANY BANK BY NEGOTIATION DRAFTS AT 30 DAYS AFTER SIGHT FOR FULL INVOICE VALUE DRAWN ON US

PARTIAL SHIPMENT：PROHIBITED

TRANSHIPMENT：ALLOWED

PORT OF LOADING：SHANGHAI

PORT OF DISCHARGE：SYDNEY

LATEST SHIPMENT DATE：2009.09.15

DESCRIPTION OF GOODS: ANGLE GRINDER, CIF SYDNEY

MS8230	542PCS	@USD23.50/PC	USD12 737.00
MS8812	1 000PCS	@USD15.00/PC	USD15 000.00
MS8804	800PCS	@USD20.40/PC	USD16 320.00
MS8803	545PCS	@USD23.20/PC	USD12 644.00
TOTAL:	2 887PCS		USD56 701.00

AS PER CONTRACT NO： 2009KMS009

DOCUMENTS REQUIRED：

*SIGNED COMMERCIAL INVOICE IN TRIPLICATE

*PACKING LIST IN TRIPLICATE

*FULL SET OF CLEAN ON BOARD MARINE BILLS OF LADING MADE OUT TO ORDER MARKED FREIGHT PREPAID NOTIFY APPLICANT

*GSP FORM A CERTIFYING THAT THE GOODS ARE OF CHINESE ORIGIN ISSUED BY COMPETENT AUTHORITIES

*INSURANCE POLICY/CERTIFICATE COVERING ALL RISKS INCLUDING WAREHOUSE TO WAREHOUSE CLAUSE UP TO FINAL DESTINATION AT SYDNEY FOR AT LEAST 110 PCT OF CIF VALUE AS PER THE CIC.

*SHIPPING ADVICES MUST BE SENT TO APPLICANT WITHIN 3 DAYS IMMEDIATELY AFTER SHIPMENT ADVISING THE INVOICE VALUE, NUMBER OF PACKAGES, GROSS AND NET WEIGHT, VESSEL NAME, BILL OF LADING NO. AND DATE, CONTRACT NO.

PRESENTATION PERIOD：10 DAYS AFTER ISSUANCE DATE OF SHIPPING DOCUMENTS BUT WITHIN THE VALIDITY OF THE CREDIT

CONFIRMATION：WITHOUT

INSTRUCTIONS：THIS CREDIT IS SUBJECT TO UNIFORM CUSTOMS A PRACTICE FOR DOCUMENTARY CREDIT ICC NO.600. THE NEGOTIATION BANK MUST FORWARD THE DRAFTS AND ALL DOCUMENTS BY REGISTERED AIRMAIL DIRECT TO US IN TWO CONSECUTIVE LOTS. UPON RECEIPT OF THE DRAFTS AND DOCUMENTS IN ORDER, WE WILL REMIT THE PROCEEDS AS INSTRUCTED BY THE NEGOTIATING BANK.

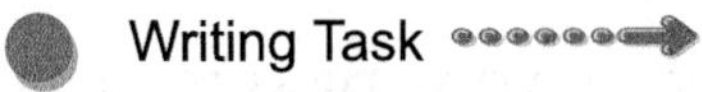

Writing Task

请根据销售合同，结合业务背景，对上述信用证进行审核，并根据审核结果撰写改证函。

Writing Guide

信用证和买卖合同是国际货物贸易中两个相互关联而又各自独立的法律文件。信用证是以买卖合同为基础开立的，其中所列的条款，从理论上说，应当与买卖合同的规定相符，这是信用证与买卖合同的关联所在。但是，信用证本身是一个独立的文件，银行与凭已开立信用证的销售合同毫无关系并不受其约束，而且银行的付款保证是以受益人提交的单据符合信用证条款为条件的，所以开证行的资信、信用证的各项内容，都关系到收汇的安全。

根据合同审核信用证，审核时不但要注意审核信用证与合同的不符之处，还要注意审核信用证自身各个条款之间有无矛盾之处。此外，对于要求修改信用证的函电，语言表述也有严格的要求。

1. 基本的信用证有关方

开证申请人，受益人，开证行，通知行，付款行，议付行，保兑行，偿付行。

2. 审证需要注意的基本内容

1）信用证本身的说明。例如信用证的种类、号码、性质、金额、使用货币及有效期、议付地点、开证申请人、受益人等。还要注意信用证是否可以撤销，可否转让，是否加保，是否循环等。

2）信用证对单据的要求。

3）保付条款。

4）对货物和运输的要求。销售合同的主要条款在这里都要体现出来。

3. 审证需重点关注的内容

一般审核信用证时，重点关注下列内容：

1）信用证两个主要当事人——开证申请人和受益人，即买方和卖方的名称是否准确无误。

2）信用证是否属于“不可撤销（Irrevocable）”信用证。

3）装运期、信用证有效期、交单期是否合理。

4）信用证到期（议付）地点是否在出口国境内。

5）信用证内容是否齐全，如单据条款、货物条款、有效期、目的港、金额等。

6）合同主要条款是否在来证中如实反映出来（品名、规格、数量、单价、总值、包装、唛头、装期、装卸港、保险等）。

7）其他要注意的问题，如：保留性条款和限制性条款及不合理要求，及其他信用证软条款；佣金和折扣是否表达正确；银行费用的分担是否合理；逻辑是否合理，如提单副本应该在装运后寄给开证申请人，装运前寄单是不合理的。

4. 要求修改信用证的函电的构成

受益人要求修改信用证的函电通常由三部分组成：

1）确认收到有关信用证，同时指出信用证中有不符点。

2）详述不符点的内容并提出如何修改。

3）要求开证申请人尽快修改信用证，以便能及时装运货物。

In international trade, the L/C and the sales contract are related to but independent of each other. They are linked because the L/C is opened on the basis of the sales contract and theoretically, its stipulations should be exact accordance with the clauses of the sales contract. However, the L/C is separated from the sales contract for the opening bank has nothing to do with the sales contract and is not bound by the contract. Moreover, the bank guarantees payment only on condition that the beneficiary's documents are line with the L/C stipulations. Therefore, the credit standing of the opening bank and the contents of the L/C can influence the secure obtainment of the payment.

In order to ensure the safe obtainment of the payment, the sellers should run a serious check on the covering L/C as soon as it arrives. Check on L/C is quite important in that it signifies a lot in carrying out our foreign trade policy, fulfilling our obligation to ship the goods, submitting the shipping documents as scheduled and making or taking delivery of the goods safely and in good time.

1. Paties Related to L/C

Applicant, beneficiary, opening bank, advising bank, paying bank, negotiating bank, confirming bank, and reimbursing bank.

Checks on the L/C can be categorized into two varieties: general terms checks and specific terms checks.

2. Key Points of General Terms Checks

1) Checks on L/C should be conducted according to our state policy.

2) Checks should be run on the credit standing of the opening bank.

3) Checks have to be held on whether or not the L/C is already in fore or bears reservation and limitation clauses.

4) Checks on the irrevocability of the L/C are quite essential.

3. Key Points of Specific Terms Checks

1) The type of L/C should be in agreement with the stipulations in the sales contract.

2) The names of the two major parties involved in the L/C, the applicant and the beneficiary must be correct and exact.

3) Check the contract number, currency, amount, the time for payment, descriptions of the goods in the L/C are whether or not the same as that stipulated in the sales contract.

4) Checks are run to ensure that the expiry date, date and place for presentation of documents and the latest date for shipment are all acceptable.

4. Parts Composing E-mails concerning L/C Amendent

Letters or e-mails concerning the L/C amendment are usually composed of three parts:

1) The beneficiary acknowledges the receipt of the covering L/C. At the same time, the beneficiary points out that there are, in the L/C, some terms and conditions different from those in the sales contract.

2) The beneficiary states in detail the discrepancies and proposes how to amend the L/C.

3) The beneficiary requests the applicant to amend the L/C as soon as possible, so that shipment can be effected in good time.

Reference E-mail

Dear Kathy,

Thank you for your L/C No. SYN88095, but we regret to say that we have found some discrepancies. Please amend the L/C as follows:

1) Partial shipment should be allowed, not prohibited.

2) Draft to be at sight instead of at 30 days after sight.

3) Presentation period should be 10 days instead of 15 days after B/L date.

Please amend the L/C immediately, so that we can make arrangements to ship the goods in good time.

Thanks and Best Regards,

Julia

Task 6 Shipment

浙江考美斯电器有限公司收到信用证修改件时已是 9 月 10 日，此时，9 月 15 日前的舱位已经无法订到，故浙江考美斯电器有限公司方面要求延迟发货，撰函如下：

Dear Kathy,

The goods you ordered are ready for shipment for a long time, but your amendment has reached us today. We contacted the shipping company and regret to tell you that we are unable to comply with your request. We have been informed that there is no space available on ships sailing from here to your port before September 15.

We are very sorry that we are unable to make shipment as stipulated. So we have to ship the goods after the stipulated time. Please amend the L/C again, extending the date of shipment and validity to September 30 and October 15 respectively.

Thanks and Best Regards,

Julia

Writing Task

请根据上述背景资料，以澳大利亚 Auto Power Co., Ltd.公司的名义给浙江考美斯电器有限公司复函，告诉对方信用证修改件已经寄出，希望能够尽早发货。

Writing Guide

在国际贸易中，最主要的运输方式是海洋运输。海洋运输条款又称“海运条款”，是贸易合同的一个重要组成部分，主要涉及货物装运条件和相互责任。在洽商外销合同时，进出口双方必须就装运时间、装运港和目的港、能否分批装运和转船转运等问题进行协商，并在合同中加以明确。要争取把合同中的装运条款订得合理、明确，以利于进出口业务的顺利开展。

Terms of Shipment include time of shipment, port of shipment/destination and transshipment/partial shipment (not) allowed.

The effectuation of shipment signifies the seller's fulfillment of the obligation to make delivery of the goods. So far as foreign trade is concerned, shipment is mostly made by ocean vessel.

The ocean B/L is an essential document in making a shipment. It presents three aspects. First, it's a receipt of the goods. Second, it's a contract for the performance of certain services upon certain conditions. Third, it serves also as evidence of ownership of the goods described.

Letters or E-mails regarding shipment are usually written for the following purposes: to urge an early shipment; to amend shipping terms; to give shipping advice; to dispatch shipping documents and so on.

Reference E-mail

Dear Julia,

Thanks for your e-mail.

We are glad to know that the goods we ordered have been ready for shipment for a long time. The amendment you mentioned was sent to you today. I'm sure you can receive it in a few days.

As our clients are in urgent need of the goods, we hope you can ship them as soon as possible. If necessary, you can ship the goods with transshipment at Hong Kong.

Best Regards,

Kathy

Task 7 Insurance

Writing Background

9 月 28 日浙江考美斯电器有限公司给中国人民保险公司上海分公司去函，要求对出口到澳大利亚的货物进行投保，函件如下：

Dear Sirs,

Please insure an original Marine Insurance Policy and 3 copies as follows:

Policy in the name of Zhejiang Calmex Electrical Appliance Co., Ltd.

Valued at US $62371.10

Per S.S. "East Wind", Sailing on September 30, 2009

Via or Transshipment at Hong Kong

Terms All Risks and War Risk .

Claim Payable at Sydney

Mark	Description of Goods	Amount
N/M	Angle Grinder	USD 56701.00

Yours sincerely,

Julia

Writing Task

请根据上述函件要求，以中国人民保险公司杭州分公司的名义给浙江考美斯电器有限公司复函。

Writing Guide

货物运输保险就是被保人或投保人在货物装运前，估计一定的投保金额向保险人或承保人（即保险公司）投保货物运输险，被保险人按保险金额、投保险别及保险费率，向保险人支付保险费并取得保险单据。被保险货物如果在运输途中遭受事故或造成损失，保险人有责任对保险险别责任范围内的损失，按保险金额及损失程度赔偿保险单据的持有人。

目前，中国人民保险公司承办的对外贸易货物运输的主保险业务包括海上运输保险、陆上运输保险、航空运输保险和邮包运输保险等，其中，业务量最大的是海上运输保险。海上运输货物保险的险别分为基本险和附加险。其中，基本险包括平安险、水渍险和一切险，责任范围从小到大。附加险又可分为一般附加险和特殊附加险。一般附加险包括偷窃提货不着险、淡水雨淋险、渗漏险、短量险、破碎险、钩损险、受潮受热险等包括特殊附加险包括战争险、罢工险等。

Insurance is a system of protection against loss. If you agree to pay certain sums—premium — periodically for a guarantee that you will be compensated under stipulated conditions for any specified loss by fire, accident, death, etc.. Since the major means of transportation in international trade is marine shipping, we'll mainly discuss marine insurance in this unit.

Generally speaking, there are basic risks and additional risks.

1) Basic risks: F.P.A.[11] (Free From Particular Average), W.A.or W.P.A.[12] (With Particular Average), All Risks[13].

2）Additional risks: General Additional Risks[14] (TPND, Leakage…), Special Additional Risks[15] (War risks, SRCC …).

There are two kinds of average:

1）General Average: It's a loss resulting from a voluntary sacrifice or expenditure, in time of peril, for the safety of hull, cargo and freight.

2）Particular Average: It means partial loss or damage accidentally caused to the ship or to a particular lot of goods.

When you want to claim, you must present the following documents to the insurance company or its agent:

① Insurance policy or certificate;

② Bill of Lading;

③ Original invoice;

④ Survey report;

⑤ Master's protest;

⑥ Statement of claim.

Reference E-mail

Dear Julia,

Insurance Policy

Policy No. 2358716038

This is to certify that the Company has issued on behalf of ZHEJIANG CALMEX ELECTRICAL APPLIANCE CO., LTD., the sum of US dollars SIXTY TWO THOUSAND THREE HUNDRED SENVENTY ONE AND POINT ONE.

Upon 2887 CARTONS ANGLE GRINDER

At & from SHANGHAI to SYDNEY via HONGKONG

Ship or vessel: S.S. "East Wind".

Sailing on or about SEPTEMBER 30, 2009.

Covering AII RISKS AND WAR RISK.

In the event of damage, it will be surveyed by the Smith Survey Company and claims are payable at SYDNEY.

This policy is issued in duplicate at SHANGHAI on the 30th day of SEPTEMBER in the year two thousand and nine.

The People's Insurance Company of China
Shanghai Branch
Manager

Specimen E-mails

(1) Establishing Business Relations 1

Dear Sirs,

We owe your name and address to the Commercial Counselor's Office of the Swedish Embassy in Beijing who has informed us that you are in the market for textiles.

We avail ourselves of this opportunity to approach you for the establishment of trade relations with you.

We are a state-operated corporation, handling both the import and export of textiles. In order to acquaint you with our business lines, we enclose a copy of our Export List covering the main items suppliable at present.

Should any of the items be of interest to you, please let us know. We shall be glad to give you our lowest quotations upon receipt of your detailed requirements.

In our trade with merchants of various countries, we always adhere to the principle of equality and mutual benefit. It is our hope to promote, by joint efforts, both trade and friendship to our mutual advantage.

We look forward to receiving your inquiries soon.

Yours faithfully,
China National Textile Import & Export Corp.
Lawrence Ma
Sales Manager

(2) Establishing Business Relations 2

Dear Sirs,

The Foreign Department of the Bank of China here has recommended your corporation as being interested in establishing business relations with Chinese company for the purpose of selling Chinese tablecloth in your country.

We sell Chinese tablecloths. They are of good quality and have fine workmanship. Chinese tablecloths are very popular in America. We would like to work with you to market them in Canada.

We are sending you under separate cover by airmail a copy of the latest catalog. Please let us know if there are any items which are of interest to you and we will send you quotations and samples.

We hope to hear from you soon.

Sincerely yours,
China National Textile Import & Export Corp.
Daphne Zhang
Manager

(3) Establishing Business Relations 3

Dear Mr. Black,

We have your name and address from http://www.alibaba.com and are glad to learn that you are selling Hand bags. As this item falls within the business scope of our company, we shall be very pleased to enter into trade relations with you.

Our company was founded in 1985, having more than 20 years of import and export experience. We specialize in light industrial products and are interested in your handbags. We are sure that the products will be very popular in our market. Would you please send us a catalogue with a price list for our reference?

We look forward to your early reply and hope that we shall be able to conclude some transactions with you in the near future.

Yours sincerely,

Guangzhou Yinghua Trading Co., Ltd.

Benjamin Zhang

Light Industrial Products Department

(4) Establishing Business Relations 4

Dear Sir or Madam,

Learning from the Commercial Counselor's Office of our Embassy in your country that you are one of the leading importers of canned foodstuffs, we have the pleasure of introducing ourselves to you as a state corporation specializing in the export of canned goods, and express our desire to enter into business relations with you.

In order to give you a general idea of our canned goods, we are sending you by separate airmail a copy of our latest catalogue. Quotations and samples will be sent to you upon receipt of your specific inquiries.

We are looking forward with interest to hearing from you.

Yours faithfully,

China National Foodstuff Import & Export Corp.

Manager

(5) Establishing Business Relations 5

Dear Mr. Lockwood,

From the September 4 issue of the International Business Daily we have learned that you are in the market for chinaware, which just falls within our business scope. We are now writing to you to establish long-term trade relations.

As a leading trading company in Shanghai and backed by more than 20 years of export experience, we have good connections with some reputable ceramics, and sufficient supplies and on-time delivery are thus guaranteed.

Enclosed please find our latest catalogue. You'll see that we can offer a wide selection of quality dinner and tea sets, ranging from the elegant Chinese traditional styles to the popular European modern designs.

In particular, we would like to inform you that we have a new line that may be most suitable for your requirements—HX series (See the attached catalogue).They are all made of first-class porcelain, decorated with hand-painted pattern, and packed in eye-catching gift cases. Most of articles are available from stock.

We are sure you will find a ready sale for our products in Canada just as other retailers have throughout Europe and USA.

Please let us know if we may be of further assistance, and we are looking forward to your specific inquiry.

Yours Sincerely,
Shanghai Huaxia Imp. & Exp. Corp.
Jeff Lee
Daily Articles Division

Encl.: a catalogue

(6) Inquiry 1

Dear Sirs,

We were impressed by the selection of sweaters that were displayed on your stand at Canton Fair last month.

We are a large chain of retailers and looking for a manufacturer who could supply us with a wide range of sweaters for the women market.

As we usually place very large orders, we would expect a 20% quantity discount and our terms of payment are normally 30 days bill of exchange, documents against payment.

If these conditions interest you, and you can meet orders of over 10,000 garments at one time, please send us your current catalogue and price list.

We hope to hear from you soon.

Yours faithfully,
Hellen

(7) Inquiry 2

Dear Sirs,

We are interested in buying large quantities of man-made gloves in all styles.

We would be obliged if you could give us a quotation per pair CIF New York, America. It would also be appreciated if you could forward samples and your price list to us.

We used to purchase these products from other sources. We may now prefer to buy from

China because we understand that you are able to supply larger quantities at more attractive prices. In addition, we have confidence in the quality of your products.

We look forward to hearing from you by return E-mail.

Sincerely,
John
Purchasing Department

(8) Reply 1

Dear Sirs,

We welcome your inquiry of 10th May and thank you for your interest in our products. A copy of our illustrated catalogue is being sent to you today, with samples of our products.

Mr. Zhang, our overseas director, will be in London early next month and will be glad to call on you. He will have with him a wide range of our manufactures, and when you see them we think you will agree that the quality of the materials used and the high standard of craftsmanship will appeal to the most selective buyers.

We also manufacture a wide range of hand-made leather bags in which we think you may be interested. They are fully illustrated in the catalogue and are of the same high quality as our gloves. Mr. Zhang will be able to show you samples when he calls.

We hope the samples will reach you in good time and look forward to your order.

Yours Faithfully,
Tom

(9) Reply 2

Dear Sirs,

We thank you for your inquiry of March 2nd and for your interest in our products. We are enclosing a copy of our illustrated catalogue and a price list giving the details you have asked for.

We believe that you will agree that our products and prices appeal to your customers. And we also allow a discount of about 5% according to the quantity ordered.

Thank you again for your interest in our products. We are looking forward to your specific inquiry and you may be assured that it will receive our prompt and careful attention.

Yours Truly,
Jane
Sales Manager

(10) Offer 1

Dear Paul,

In reply to your E-mail yesterday, we have pleasure in enclosing a detailed quotation for bathroom showers.

Besides those advertised in the Builders' Journal, our illustrated catalogue enclosed also shows various types of bathroom fittings and the sizes available. Most types can be supplied from stock. We can deliver them within 60 days.

Our clients in Europe have found our equipment easy to install and attractive in appearance. Naturally all parts are replaceable, and our quotation includes prices of spare parts. We can allow a 2% discount on all orders of US$10 000 in value and over, and a 3% on orders exceeding US$20 000.

Any orders you place with us will be processed promptly.

Yours Sincerely,
Mary Dong
Sales Manager

(11) Offer 2

Dear Mary,

In reply to your E-mail of December 20, 2009, we are making you the following offer:

Commodity: Phoenix Brand Men's T-Shirts.

Specifications: dyed, short sleeves, pure silk, long collar, full open front, one chest pocket.

Colours: white series (Sample 1); blue series (Sample 2,3,4); yellow series (Sample 5,6,7).

Size: S1, S2, S3; M1, M2, M3; L1, L2, L3, XL.

Packing: Each piece in a polybag, a dozen in one carton box, 10 dozens in a wooden case.

Quantity: 3 000 dozens.

Price: USD20 per dozen CIF Vancouver.

Shipment: April, 2010 allowing transshipment and partial shipment.

Payment: By 100% confirmed irrevocable letter of credit in our favor available by draft at sight to reach the Sellers one month before the date of shipment and remain valid for negotiation at Bank of China till the 15th day after shipment.

Under separate cover, we have already sent you samples of various colours and sizes. If you find our offer agreeable, please fax us acceptance for our confirmation.

Yours Sincerely,
Jane
Sales Manager

(12) Counter-offer 1

Dear Mr. Li,

We acknowledge receipt of both your offer of May 5 and the samples of Men's Shirts, and thank you for these.

While appreciating the good quality of your shirts, we find your price is rather too high for the market we wish to supply.

We have also to point out that the Men's Shirts are available in our market from several European manufacturers. All of them are at prices from 15% to 20% below yours.

Such being the case, we have to ask you to consider if you can make reduction in your price, say 10%. As our order would be worth around USD100 000, you may think it worthwhile to make a concession.

We await with keen interest your immediate reply.

Yours Faithfully,
John Brown
Purchasing Manager

(13) Counter-offer 2

Dear Mr. Zhao,

Re: "D. D." Raincoats

Thank you for your E-mail of June 25 offering us your "D.D." brand raincoats.

To be candid with you, we like your raincoats, but your prices appear to be on the high side as compared with those of other makes. It is understood that to accept the prices you quoted would leave us little or no margin of profit on our sales. As you know, Jordan is a developing country. Its principal demand is for articles in the medium price range.

We appreciate your prompt response to our inquiry and would like to take this opportunity to conclude some transactions with you. We would, therefore, suggest that you make some allowance, say 10% on your quoted prices so as to enable us to introduce your products to our customers. If, however, you cannot do so, then we shall have no alternative but to leave the business as it is.

For your information, some parcels from Hong Kong have been sold here at a much lower price. We hope you will consider our counter-offer favorably and let us have your acceptance by fax. It may interest you to know that once you have opened up a market here, you would have every advantage of developing a beneficial trade in the Gulf.

Yours Sincerely,
Sun Trading Co., Ltd.
Jones
Manager

(14) Counter-offer 3

Dear Mr. Jones,

Re: Chemical Fertilizer

We thank you for your E-mail offering us 500 metric tons of the subject goods at US$ 500 per metric ton CFR Shanghai on usual terms.

In reply, we regrettably state that our end-users here find your price too high and out of line with the prevailing market level. Information indicates that some parcels of Japanese make have been sold at the level of US$ 460 per metric ton.

Such being the case, it is impossible for us to persuade our end-users to accept your price, as the material of similar quality is easily obtainable at a much lower price. Should you be prepared to reduce your limit by, say 10%, we might come to terms.

It is in view of our long-standing business relationship that we make you such a counter-offer. As the market is declining, we hope you will consider our counter-offer most favorably and send us acceptance by E-mail as soon as you can.

Yours Faithfully,
Universal Trading Co., Ltd.
Matin Huang
Purchasing Manager

(15) Acceptance 1

Dear Mr. Li,

Your quotation of July 20 has been accepted and we are glad to place our order No. 123 as follows:

COMMODITY	ART No.	PACKING	CTNS/20FCL	CIFC3HAMBURG
TOYS	KB001	12PCS/CTN	1200CTNS	USD6/PC
	KB002	12PCS/CTN	1300CTNS	USD5/PC
	KB003	12PCS/CTN	1100CTNS	USD8/PC

Other terms and conditions are the same as we agreed before.

As this is the first transaction we have concluded, your cooperation would be very much appreciated. Please send us your sales confirmation in duplicate for counter-signature.

Best Regards,
Paul
Purchasing Department

(16) Acceptance 2

Dear Mr. Zhang,

Thank you for your quotation.

Although we think your prices seem to be on the high side, in consideration of the very pleasant cooperation we have had with you, we hope to inform you that your quotation dated September 18, 2009 has been booked and we are glad to place our order No. AB23 as follows:

COMMODITY	MODEL	PACKING	CARTONS PER 20 FCL	CIF3%HAMBURG (USD)
CAR SPEAKERS	PY-1009	10PAIRS/CTN	6 000	3.20/PAIR
	PY-1008	5PAIRS/CTN	3 000	16.00/PAIR

Other terms and conditions remain the same as we agreed in our previous mails.

We trust that everything is now in order and you will be able to ship the goods on time. Should your goods prove to be satisfactory upon arrival, we are confident that large orders will be followed. When the goods are ready for shipment, please send us shipping advice by E-mail to facilitate our making the necessary arrangement.

We are looking forward to your Sales Conformation and thank you in advance.

Yours Sincerely,
Stephen Jones
Sunlit Trade Corp.

(17) Payment 1

Dear Mr. Jones,

With reference to our Sales Confirmation No.825 dated August 10, 2009, we regret to say that your letter of credit has not yet reached us up to the time of writing. This has caused us much inconvenience as we have already made preparations for shipment according to the stipulations of the said Sales Confirmation.

You must be aware that the terms and conditions of a contract once signed should be strictly observed, failure to abide by them will mean violation of contract. If you refer to our Sales Confirmation, you will see the clause reading:

"The Buyer shall establish the covering Letter of Credit before 31st August, 2009. If not, the Seller reserves the right to rescind the contract without further notice."

The goods you ordered have been ready for quite some time and the demand for them has been so great that we find it hard to keep them for you any longer. However, in consideration of our long friendly business relations, we are prepared to wait for your L/C, which must reach us not later than October 5, 2009. If we again fail to receive your L/C in time, we shall cancel our Sales Confirmation and ask you to refund to us the storage charges we have paid on your behalf.

Your cooperation in this respect will be appreciated.

Sincerely,
Hellen

(18) Payment 2

Dear Mr. Brown,

We have received your L/C No.121/99 issued by the Yemen Bank for Reconstruction & Development for the amount of US$ 19 720 covering 1 600 dozen Men's Shirts. After reviewing the L/C, we find that transshipment and partial shipment are not allowed.

As direct steamers to your port are difficult to find, we have to ship via Hong Kong. As to partial shipment, it would be our mutual benefit because we could ship immediately whatever we have on hand instead of waiting for the whole lot to be completed.

We, therefore, write to ask you to amend the L/C reading: "TRANSSHIPMENT AND PARTIAL SHIPMENT ALLOWED".

We shall be glad if you see to it that amendment is faxed without any delay, as our goods have been packed ready for shipment for quite some time.

Sincerely,
Hellen

(19) Payment 3

Dear Mr. White,

We thank you for your L/C. We are sorry that owing to some delay on the part of our suppliers, we are not able to get the goods ready before the end of this month. Please extend the shipment date and validity in you L/C No.1415 to May 15 and 31 respectively.

It is expected that the consignment will be ready for shipment in the early part of May and we are arranging to ship it on S.S. "East Wind" sailing from Dalian on or about May10.

We are looking forward to receiving your amendment of the above L/C thus enabling us to effect shipment of the goods in question.

We thank you for your cooperation.

Sincerely,
Hellen

(20) Shipment 1

Dear Ms. Ni,

RE: Order No. 9953

We refer to the contract No. 632 covering 500 dozen blouses. We wish to remind you that we have had no news from you about shipment of the goods.

As we mentioned in our last E-mail, we are in urgent need of the goods and we may be compelled to seek an alternative source of supply.

Under the circumstances, it is not possible for us to extend further our letter of credit No. 16852, which expires on 21 August. Please understand how serious and urgent it is for us to resolve this matter.

We look forward to receiving your shipping advice by E-mail within the next five days.

Yours Faithfully,
H. Koppermann
Managing Director

(21) Shipment 2

Dear Sirs,

Thank you for your E-mail of 20 May inquiring about the shipment of your order under

Contract No. 4632.

Please accept my apology for the delay which has been caused by the unavailability of shipping space from Bombay to London.

The matter was, however, in hand and your consignment was shipped yesterday on board S.S. "Huangpu" which is sailing directly to London.

We enclose one set of shipping documents comprising:

1) One non-negotiable copy of the B/L;

2) Commercial invoice in duplicate;

3) One copy of the certificate of guarantee;

4) One copy of the certificate of quantity;

5) One copy of the insurance policy.

We are glad that we have been able to execute your order as contracted. We trust the goods will reach you in time for the winter selling season and prove to be entirely satisfactory. We will ensure that you receive our prompt and careful attention at all times.

Yours Faithfully,
Tom
Sales Manager

(22) Shipment 3

Dear Sirs,

Thank you for your E-mail of 20 March requesting earlier delivery of goods under your Purchase Contract No. 954.

We have contacted the shipping company and regret to tell you that we are unable to comply with your request. We have been informed that there is no available space on ships sailing from here to your port before 5 April.

We are very sorry that we are unable to advance shipment. We will, however, do everything possible to ensure that the goods are shipped within the contracted time.

Yours Faithfully,
Tony
Manager

(23) Insurance 1

Dear Sirs,

Please insure us against All Risks USD 110 000, value of 6 000 sets of "Butterfly" Sewing Machines shipped at Shanghai, on board S.S. "Yellow River", sailing for New York on July 10th. Please send us the policy, together with a note for the charges.

Sincerely,
Tony

(24) Insurance 2

Dear Sirs,

Regarding your instructions dated July 8, we have insured your shipment of 6 000 sets of "Butterfly" Sewing Machines shipped at Shanghai on board S.S. "Yellow River", sailing for New York on July 10th, as per the policy enclosed. Please remit USD 1 700 to our account for this policy by bank check.

Sincerely,

Tom

(25) Insurance 3

Dear Sirs,

This is in reply to your E-mail of September 4 regarding insurance:

Your customer's request for insurance coverage up to the inland city is acceptable on condition that such extra premium is for his account.

Second, we cannot grant you insurance coverage for 150% of the invoice value, because the contract stipulates that insurance is to be covered for 110% of invoice value.

We trust the above information serves your purpose. Meanwhile, we await your reply.

Sincerely,

John

(26) Insurance 4

Dear Sirs,

Re: Your Order No. 956 for 600-Carton Toys

We have received your E-mail requesting us to effect insurance on the captioned shipment for your account.

We are pleased to inform you that we have covered the above shipment with The People's Insurance Company of China against All Risks for USD 6 500.00. The policy is being prepared accordingly and will be forwarded to you by the end of the week together with our debit note for the premium.

For your information, we are making arrangements to ship the 600 cartons of toys by S.S. "East Wind", sailing on or about the 15th of August.

Yours Sincerely,

Bury Li

Notes

1. ISO 9001：ISO 9001 是 ISO 9000 族标准所包括的质量管理体系核心标准之一。ISO 9000 族标准是国际标准化组织（ISO）在 1994 年提出的，是指“由 ISO/TC176”（国际标准化组织品质管理和品质保证技术委员会）制定的国际标准。

ISO 9001 用于证实组织具有提供满足顾客要求和适用法规要求的产品的能力。随着商品经济的不断扩大和日益国际化，ISO 9001 认证有利于提高产品信誉、减少重复检验、削弱和消除贸易技术壁垒，维护生产者、经销者、用户和消费者的权益。ISO 认证不受产销双方经济利益支配，公正、科学，作为顾客对供方质量体系审核的依据，证明企业有满足其订购产品技术要求的能力，是各国对产品和企业进行质量评价和监督的通行证。

凡是通过 ISO 认证的企业，表明其在各项管理系统整合上达到了国际标准，能持续稳定地向顾客提供预期和满意的合格产品。

2. UL 是保险商试验所（Underwriter Laboratories Inc.）的英文简写。UL 安全试验所是美国最权威的，也是世界上从事安全试验和鉴定的较大的民间机构。它主要从事产品的安全认证和经营安全证明业务，其最终目的是为市场得到具有相当安全水准的商品，为人身健康和财产安全得到保障作出贡献。

UL 始建于 1894 年，初始阶段主要靠防火保险部门提供资金维持运作。直到 1916 年，UL 才完全自立。经过近百年的发展，UL 已成为世界知名的认证机构，其自身具有一整套严密的组织管理体制、标准开发和产品认证程序。UL 是由一个由安全专家、政府官员、消费者、教育界、公用事业、保险业及标准部门的代表组成的理事会，日常工作由总裁、副总裁处理。目前，UL 在美国本土有五个实验室，总部设在芝加哥北部的小镇诺斯布鲁克（Northbrook），同时在中国台湾和香港分别设立了相应的实验室。

3. CE：在欧盟市场，“CE”属强制性认证标志，无论欧盟内部企业生产的产品，还是其他国家生产的产品，要想在欧盟市场上自由流通，就必须加贴“CE”标志，以表明产品符合欧盟《技术协调与标准化新方法》指令的基本要求。这是欧盟对产品提出的一种强制性要求。因此，“CE”标志一向被制造商视为打开并进入欧洲市场的护照。

4. EMC：EMC 是 Electro Magnetic Compatibility 的缩写，即电磁兼容。其定义为“设备和系统在其电磁环境中能正常工作且不对环境中任何事物构成不能承受的电磁干扰的能力”。该定义包含两个层面的意思。首先，该设备应能在一定的电磁环境下正常工作，即该设备应具备一定的电磁抗扰度（EMS）；其次，该设备自身产生的电磁场不能对其他电子产品造成过大的影响，即电磁干扰（EMI）。

20 世纪末欧盟规定，从 1996 年 1 月 1 日起，所有电气电子产品必须通过 EMC 认证，加贴 CE 标志后才能在欧盟市场上销售。

5. CSA：CSA 是加拿大标准协会（Canadian Standards Association）的简称，成立于 1919 年，是加拿大首家专门制定工业标准的非营利性机构。 CSA 是加拿大最大的安全认证机构，也是世界上最著名的安全认证机构之一。它能对机械、建材、电器、电脑设备、办公设备、环保设备、医疗防火安全设备、运动器械及娱乐工具等方面的所有类型的产品提供安全认证。

目前 CSA 已为遍布全球的数千厂商提供了认证服务，每年有上亿件附有 CSA 标志的产品在北美市场销售。

6. GS: GS 的全称是“Geprufte Sicherheit”（德语，安全性已认证），也有“Germany Safety”（德国安全）的意思。GS 认证是以德国设备与产品安全法（GPSG）为依据，按照欧盟统一标准（EN）或德国工业标准（DIN）进行检测的一种自愿性认证，是欧洲市场公认的安全认证标志。贴有 GS 标志表示该产品的使用安全性已经通过具公信力的独立机构的测试。

GS 标志虽然不属法律强制要求，但是它确实能在产品发生故障而造成意外事故时，使制造商受到严格的德国（欧洲）产品安全法的约束。所以 GS 标志具有强有力的市场吸引力，能增强顾客的信心及购买欲望，一个拥有 GS 标志的电器在市场上可能会较一般产品有更大的竞争力。

7. CB：CB 是英文 Certification Bodies' Schemer 的缩写，中文意思为认证机构体系，即国际电工委员会电工产品测试证书互认体系。CB 体系（CB Scheme- IECEE）是国际电工委员会电工产品合格测试与认证组织关于电工产品安全测试报告和安全测试证书相互认可的一个国际体系。CB 体系的目的是协调国家标准与 IEC 标准，使贸易更加容易，并且通过国际范围内认证机构之间的合作，使产品制造商得到理想的一站式服务：一种产品、一次测试、一个标志。

CB 体系是一个真正意义上有关电子电器产品的安全报告互相认可体系。它是一个参与其中的国家或认证组织的多边协议，一个制造商持有其中一个成员机构（NCB）颁发的 CB 测试报告及证书，就可以获得 CB 体系内其他成员的认可。目前国际上已有 40 多个国家参加了国际电工委员会电工产品合格测试与认证组织，成为可以颁发 CB 证书并相互认可的国家认证机构即 NCB。中国质量认证中心（CQC）是我国唯一的 NCB。

CB 体系运作的先决条件是国家标准与相应的 IEC 标准的合理协调，如果某些成员的国家标准与 IEC 标准不完全相同，则需要向其他成员明示。CB 体系以 CB 证书表明有代表性的样品已成功通过适当的测试，符合相应的 IEC 标准。

8. NOM：NOM（NORMAS OFFICIALES MEXICANAS）是墨西哥安全认证标志，用以表示产品符合相关的 NOM 标准。NOM 标志适用于电信及信息技术设备、家庭电气用品、灯具和其他对健康及安全具有潜在威胁的产品。无论在墨西哥本地制造的还是进口的产品，均需符合相关的 NOM 标准及产品标注规定，进入墨西哥的产品必须经过 NOM 认证。

根据墨西哥法律，墨西哥有两种验证单位可核发 NOM 标志：

1）NOM NYCE：验证范围包括所有的电子和资讯产品及资料处理设备，但不包括家电用品（微波炉除外）；

2）NOM ANCE：验证范围包括所有的电器和类似产品（如家电产品）。

9. SAA：澳大利亚国际标准公司（Standards Australia International Limited）是澳大利亚唯一的标准认证机构。无论是进口还是在澳大利亚当地组装的电器产品，在进入澳大利亚市场销售前，首先要通过澳大利亚国际标准公司的认证，即 SAA 认证。

检验机构通过对电器的破坏性试验，如在高温情况下，不间断地超负荷使用电器，检查电器的安全性能；对洗衣机的外表进行漏水试验，检查是否漏电；对电器的电源插座进行非正常使用，看是否存在安全隐患等。

SAA 主要有两种标志，一种是形式认可，一种是标准标志。目前国内申请 SAA 认证有两种途径，一是通过 CB 测试报告申请，若没有 CB 测试报告，也可以直接申请。

10. CCC：3C 认证是英文"China Compulsory Certification"（中国强制性产品认证）的缩写，也是我国对强制性产品认证使用的统一标志。它是我国政府按照世贸组织有关协议和国际通行规则，为保护广大消费者人身和动植物生命安全、保护环境和国家安全，依照法律法规实施的一种产品合格评定制度。其主要特点：国家公布统一的目录，确定统一适用的国家标准、技术规则和实施程序，制定统一的标志标识，规定统一的收费标准。

凡列入强制性产品认证目录的产品，必须经国家指定的认证机构认证合格、取得相关证书并加施认证标志后，方能出厂、进口、销售和在经营服务场所使用。目前，中国公布的首批必须通过强制性认证的产品共有 19 大类 132 种，主要包括电线电缆、低压电器、信息技术设备、安全玻璃、消防产品、机动车辆轮胎、乳胶制品等。

11. F.P.A.： 平安险（Free from Particular Average，简称 FPA），其承保责任范围包括：由于自然灾害和意外事故而导致的货物全部损失；由于运输工具遭受意外事故造成的货物全部或部分损失；在运输工具已经发生意外事故的情况下，货物在此前后又在海上遭受自然灾害所造成的部分损失；在装卸或转运时由于一件或数件整件货物落海造成的全部或部分损失；共同海损的牺牲、分摊以及救助费用、施救费用等。

12. W.P.A.： 水渍险（With Particular Average，简称 WPA），其承保责任范围除包括上述平安险的各项责任外，保险人还负责被保险货物由于恶劣气候、雷电、海啸、地震、洪水等自然灾害所造成的部分损失。

13. All Risks： 一切险，其承保责任范围除包括水渍险的各项承保责任外，保险人还负责被保险货物在运输途中由于一般外来风险所致的全部或部分损失。

在上述三种基本险（F.P.A.、W.P.A.及 All Risks）中，保险条款还规定了除外责任。所谓除外责任（Exclusion）是指保险公司明确规定不予承保的损失和费用。我国《海运货物保险条款》对除外责任的规定主要包括：被保险人的故意行为或过失造成的损失；属于发货人责任引起的损失；保险责任开始前，被保险货物已存在的品质不良或数量短差所造成的损失；被保险货物的自然损耗、本质缺陷、特性以及市价跌落、运输延迟所造成的损失或费用；属于海洋运输货物战争险条款和货物运输罢工险条款规定的责任范围和除外责任。

14. General Additional Risks： 一般附加险有下列 11 种险别：偷窃、提货不着险（Theft, Pilferage and Non-Delivery Risk, T.P.N.D.）；淡水雨淋险（Fresh Water and Rain Damage Risk, F.W.R.D.）；渗漏险（Leakage Risk）；短量险（Shortage Risk）；混杂、玷污险（Intermixture and Contamination Risk）；碰损、破碎险（Clash and Breakage Risk）；串味险（Taint of Odour Risk）；受潮受热险（Sweat and Heating Risk）；钩损险（Hook Damage Risk）；包装破裂险（Breakage of Packing Risk）；锈损险（Rust Risk）。

15. Special Additional Risks： 特殊附加险主要指战争险（War Risk）和罢工险（Strikes Risk）。此外还有进口关税险（Import Duty Risk）、舱面险（On Deck Risk）、黄曲霉素险（Aflatoxin Risk）、拒收险（Rejection Risk）、交货不到险（Failure to Deliver Risk）、出口货物到香港（包括九龙在内）或澳门存仓火险责任扩展条款（Fire Risk Extension Clause For Storage of Cargo at Destination HongKong, Including Kowloon or Macao，简称 F.R.E.C）等。战争险保险责任的起讫采用的是保险人只负责水面风险的原则，即从货物装上海轮或驳船时开始至货物运抵目的港卸离海轮为止。如果不卸离海轮，则以货物到达目的港当日午夜起 15 天为限。

Important Words and Phrases

1. business scope	经营范围
e.g.business relations	商务关系，业务关系
conclude a business	达成交易
2. Counsellor's Office	商务参赞处
3. cover	信封
e.g.under the same cover	随信寄上
under separate cover	另寄
4. enclose	封入（表示附在某信封中）
5. Energy Saving Lamps	节能灯
6. fall within our business scope	在我们的业务范围之内
7. for your consideration/ reference	供你方考虑/参考
8. to enter into business relations/ to establish business relations（relationship）	建立业务关系
9. seek for	寻找
10. specialize in	专门经营
11. to be in the market for sth.	要购买……
12. proforma invoice	形式发票
13. R&D	研发
14. account	账户，账目，账款
e.g.be one's account, for the account of sb.	由某人负担
on account of	由于
to take…into account	把……考虑在内
accountant	会计师
15. Angle Grinders	角向磨光机
16. be in stock（out of stock）	有（无）存货
17. commission	佣金
18. conclude a transaction/ come to terms come to business/ close a bargain/ close a deal	达成交易
19. counter-offer	还盘
20. counter-signature/countersign	会签
21. Cut-off Machines	切割机
22. discount	折扣
23. in duplicate	一式两份
24. In view of…	鉴于……
25. L/C at sight	即期信用证

26. MOQ（Minimum Order Quantity）	最低订货数量
27. on the high side	偏高
28. out of line with…	与……不一致
in line with…	与……一致
29. price list	价格单
30. purchase order	购货单
to place an order with sb. for sth.	向某人订购某货物
31. quotation	报价单
32. Random Orbit Sanders	圆板摆动式沙光机
33. Sales Confirmation	销售确认书
34. Silk Bloting Cloth	丝绢筛布
35. stone/concrete	混凝土
36. to sign and return a copy of … for one's file	签退一份……供某人存档
37. VAT（Value-Added Tax）	增值税
38. to advance shipment	提前装运
39. to advise（inform, notify）sb.	告诉、通知某人
40. to be airmailed	空（航）邮
41. to be permitted	允许
42. to be ready for shipment	准备发货
43. to book shipping space	订舱位
44. to effect shipment	装运
45. to mark	刷唛
46. to postpone shipment	延迟装运
47. to ship goods by S.S.（M.V.）	由 S.S.（M.V.）装运货物
48. transshipment	转运
49.coverage	承保险别（总称），保险范围；投保额
50. insure sb. against…	为某人投保……险
51. premium	保险费；溢价，额外价钱
52. to arrange（effect, cover）insurance	投保
53. to insure…with…	向……投保……

Useful Expressions

1. Through courtesy of Mr. Freemen, we are given to understand that you are the leading importer of electric goods in your area and wish to enter into business relations with you.

2. Your company has been introduced to us by Universal Trading Co., Ltd. as a prospective buyer of electric appliances. We wish to inform you that we specialize in this line and hope to enter into trade relations with you.

3. We have your name and address from the Commercial Counselor's Office of our Embassy in the U.K. who has informed us that you are in the market for Chinese goods.

4. We write to introduce ourselves as one of the leading exporters of chinaware.

5. We have the pleasure to introduce ourselves to you with the hope of establishing business relations with you.

6. To acquaint you with the light industrial goods we handle, we are sending you, by separate airmail, several pamphlets for your reference.

7. We are willing to establish business relations with your company on the basis of equality and mutual benefit.

8. We enclose a copy of our catalogue for your reference and hope that you would contact us if any item is interest to you.

9. We are the largest food trading company in China, and have offices and representatives in all major cities and towns in China.

10. We are glad to inform you that we are interested in hand-made gloves in a variety of genuine leather.

11. While appreciating the good quality of your shirts, we find your price is rather too high for the market we wish to supply.

12. Such being the case, we have to ask you to consider if you can make reduction in your price, say 10%.

13. To be candid with you, we like your raincoats, but your prices appear to be on the high side as compared with those of other makes.

14. It is understood that to accept the prices you quoted would leave us little or no margin of profit on our sales.

15. We hope you will consider our counter-offer favorably and let us have your acceptance by fax.

16. Much to our regret, as your price is out of line with the market level, it is difficult for us to accept it.

17. In reply, we very much regret to state that our end-users here find your price too high and out of line with the prevailing market level.

18. Unfortunately we cannot accept your offer. The prices you quoted are much higher than those of other manufacturers.

19. We do not see any advantage in your quotation, and would like to know whether you have any better price to offer.

20. Our counter-offer is well founded and workable. We can also offer a 10% discount for orders over 10 000 pieces.

21. We have cut the price to the limit. We regret, therefore, being unable to comply with your request for any further reduction.

22. We are sorry that the difference/gap between our prices and your counter-offer is too

wide. The best we can do is 5% off.

23. With reference to the faxes exchanged between us in the last few days, we are pleased to have been able to finalize the following transaction with you.

24. After long and friendly discussing, we have now concluded the business.

25. It is in view of our long-standing business relationship that we accept your counter-offer.

26. We are pleased to enclose herewith our contract No.3578 in two originals for your counter-signature. Please send one copy back to us at your earlist convenience.

27. We hope this initial deal will result in future transactions between us.

28. A good beginning makes a good ending. We hope that from now on we will enjoy business relations that are profitable to both of us.

29. Although your quotation is somewhat higher, we will accept it on the same terms as before with the view to encouraging business.

30. We have been able to confirm the following order with you at your revised price.

31.The goods under S/C No. 9827 have been ready for quite some time. Please have the Letter of Credit opened with the least possible delay.

32. In spite of our repeated requests, still we have not received your letter of credit up to now. Please open the credit by cable immediately; otherwise, we cannot effect shipment in January.

33. Please amend by telex L/C No. 3256 as allowing transshipment and partial shipment.

34. Please delete from the L/C the clause, "All bank commissions and charges are for beneficiary's account".

35. We trust that you will make all necessary arrangements to deliver the goods in time.

36. We hope that by the time you receive this letter/e-mail, you will have the goods ready for shipment.

37. Please make your best efforts to get the goods dispatched with the least possible delay.

38. It is stipulated that shipment is to be made before the end of this month; however, we shall appreciate it if you will arrange to ship the goods at an earlier date.

39. Your failure to deliver the goods within the stipulated time has greatly inconvenienced us.

40. We take pleasure in notifying you that the goods under S/C No. 295 have been dispatched by M/V "Greenwood" sailing on March 13, 2010 for Hong Kong.

41. Taking into consideration the transport condition at your end, we have improved our packing so as to avoid damage to the goods. Most of our buyers do not want to insure against the Risk of Breakage for this article.

42. We have insured against W.P.A. and War Risk at 110% of the invoice value.

43. This is in reply to your E-mail of September 4 regarding insurance.

44. Your customer's request for insurance coverage up to the inland city is acceptable on condition that such extra premium is for his account.

45. Please cover (insure) the goods With Particular Average.

46. As our order was placed on CIF basis, the insurance is to be arranged by you.

47. Insurance is to be effected by the sellers against All Risks for 110% of the invoice value with the People's Insurance Company of China.

48. The premium varies with the extent of insurance. Should additional risks be covered, the extra premium would be for buyers' account.

Exercises

1. 甜蜜卫浴公司（Sweet Shower Equipment Co.）是一家专业卫浴生产企业，以电脑蒸汽房、按摩浴缸、淋浴房、陶瓷卫生洁具和浴室柜等五大类卫浴产品生产为主，涉及配套产品开发的多元化产品线。

公司自成立以来，始终坚持“缔造尊贵的美学卫浴空间”的企业使命，弘扬“团结、务实、创新”的企业精神，致力于为广大客户提供高质量的产品和服务。“甜蜜”品牌目前已深入人心，在全国共有 10 多个自营店，200 多个经销商以及完善的售后服务体系，销售网络覆盖国内 100 多个大中城市，产品远销美国、澳大利亚、英国及中东各地。联系方式：

电话：86-579-82265305　传真：86-579-82265416

邮箱：sweet@hotmail.com

2009 年 3 月，甜蜜卫浴公司业务人员从阿里巴巴商务网站上了解到美国兄弟公司（America Brothers Co.）正在求购卫浴产品。其具体联络方式：

Mr. Johnson

Purchasing Division

America Brothers Co.

Tel No.: 001-907-2488977　Fax No.: 001-907-2488967

E-mail: Brother@163.com

请给 America Brothers Co.去函，表达与之建立业务关系的热切愿望，并随寄卫浴系列的商品目录。

2. Write to Brown & Sons at 50 Cannan Street, London, E.C.6, telling them that you wish to enter into business relations with them, with the following particulars:

1）Learn them through the Internet;

2）The main line of your business is exporting chinaware.

3. 有一天，华信公司业务员在阿里巴巴商务网站上看到澳大利亚一家公司销售的羊毛衫，款式新颖、美观大方，非常感兴趣，于是想采购一批在国内销售。

澳大利亚公司的具体联络方式：

Mr. Reed

Sales Department

Universal Trading Co., Ltd.

E-mail: cardigan@hotmail.com

请以华信公司业务员的身份给澳大利亚公司发一封邮件，希望与之建立业务关系，并对几款感兴趣的羊毛衫作具体询盘。

4. 假设你在阿里巴巴商务网站上看到加拿大 Fashion Wear 公司有意从中国购买一批领带，而这正好是你公司的经营范围，请给对方发一封建交函，内容包括：

1）你是从哪里得知对方信息的（the source of your information）；

2）你写信的目的（your intention of writing the letter）；

3）介绍你公司的情况（包括业务范围）（your company profile, including business scope）；

4）表达你的期盼（your expectation）。

5. 请根据以下内容编写一段对话。

Commodity: Lipstick

Price: US $7/PC CIF Vancouver

Quantity: 200 PCS

Payment: by irrevocable L/C at sight

Counter-offer: US$5/PC

The buyer asks for a 5% reduction in the price. The seller refuses to consider any reduction, but gives a 2% commission. Finally they conclude the business.

6. 假设你是英国 TOM'S GARMENT COMPANY 的采购部经理，2010 年 2 月来义乌参加小商品博览会，对海浪制衣有限公司生产的睡衣很感兴趣。请以 TOM'S GARMENT COMPANY 采购部经理的身份写一封询盘函，内容包括以下四个方面。

1）感兴趣的睡衣型号：MJ1167、MQ9454、MK6623。

2）MOQ 为多少？

3）请报 FOB 上海的价格。

4）请附上样本。

7. 2010 年 3 月 12 日，加拿大 TAT 公司收到了浙江纺织有限公司发来的下列报盘函。

Dear Sirs,

Thank you for your E-mail of March10, in which you inquire about our woolen blanket. We are pleased to make you an offer, subject to our final confirmation, as follows:

Commodity: "Great Wall" Brand Woolen Blanket No. 45.

Specifications: Size: 182cm×213 cm; Background Color: Red.

Quantity: 1500 pcs.

Price: US$ 200/piece CIF Vancouver.

Shipment: During July, 2010.

Payment: By 100% confirmed, irrevocable letter of credit in our favor payable by draft at sight to reach us one month before the date of shipment and remain valid for negotiation in China till the 15th day after shipment.

Yours Truly,
Catharine Zhang
Sales Manager

请以 TAT 公司采购部业务员的名义对该报盘进行还盘，要求对方降价 5%。

8. 假设你是莱佛士纺织品公司（Raffles Textile Co., Ltd.）的业务员，收到了来自新加坡 FOX 公司的订单，请根据订单的内容起草一份销售合同。

Dear Ms. Chen,

Thank you for your E-mail of 12th June sending us patterns of silk bolting cloth. We find both quality and prices satisfactory and are pleased to give you an order for the following items on the understanding that they will be supplied from current stock at the prices named.

Pattern No.	Quantity	Prices (net) CIF Singapore
69	20 yards	USD 35 cents/yard
34	35 yards	USD 29 cents/yard
28	50 yards	USD 55 cents/yard

We expect to find a good market for these silk bolting cloths and hope to place further and larger orders with you in the near future.

Our usual terms of payment are cash against documents and we hope they will be acceptable to you.

Please send us your conformation of sales in duplicate.

Sincerely Yours,
Maria Kuka
Purchasing Division

9. Check the terms set forth in L/C No. 85625 with the contents of the under mentioned S/C No. 154 to see what discrepancies exist between them and then write an E-mail requesting the buyer to make the necessary amendments.

THE CHARTERED BANK

Singapore

L/C No.85625

Date:

To: China National Import & Export Corp. Shanghai Branch

Dear Sirs,

You are hereby authorized to draw on Hua Feng Trading Co., Singapore for a sum not exceeding USD 7 850.00 CIF (Say US Dollars Seven Thousand Eight Hundred and Fifty only) available by your draft, drawn in duplicate, on them at sight, accompanied by the following documents:

1）3 non-negotiable copies of clean shipped on board B/L, marked "Freight prepaid";

2）Signed Invoice in triplicate;

3）Certificate of Origin in duplicate;

4）Insurance Policy in duplicate covering WPA & War Risk for full invoice value plus 10%;

5）Evidencing shipment from Shanghai to Singapore of the following merchandise;

6）500 dozen T-shirts as per S/C No. 1023 dated June 15, 2008.

7) Condition of Shipment:

① Transshipment is prohibited;

② Partial shipments are permitted.

This credit expires on August 18, 2008 and is subject to the Uniform Customs & Practice for Documentary Credits *2007* Revision) International Chamber of Commerce Publication No. 600.

Yours Sincerely,
THE CHARTERED BANK
Singapore
Chief Accountant

SALES CONFIRMATION

No.: 154
Date: June 15, 2008

The Seller: China National Import & Export Corp. Shanghai Branch

The Buyer: Hua Feng Trading Co. Singapore

The undersigned seller and buyer have agreed to close the following transaction, according to the terms and conditions stipulated below:

Commodity & Specifications	Quantity	Unit Price & Terms	Total Amount
Printed T-shirts: designs & color at seller's option		CIF Singapore	
Large size	250 doz.	USD 21.00	USD 5 250.00
Medium size	150 doz.	USD 15.00	USD 2 250.00
Small size	100 doz.	USD 12.50	USD 1 250.00
Total:	500 doz.		USD 8 750.00

Total value: USD 8 750. 00;

Shipment: During July/August 2008;

Payment: By 100% confirmed & Irrevocable L/C to be available by sight draft, reaching the seller 30 days before the month of shipment, remaining valid for negotiation in China for another 21 days after the prescribed time of shipment, allowing transshipment & partial shipments.

Destination: Singapore.

Insurance: To be effected by the seller at 110% of invoice value covering WPA & War Risk as per China Insurance Clauses (C.I.C.).

The Seller
Signature

The Buyer
Signature

10. 上海华夏进出口公司收到外商信用证已经是 9 月底，审核后要求加拿大 James Brown & Sons 公司修改该信用证，而修改件 10 月 20 日还未到达。此时，10 月底的舱位已经无法订到，因此上海华夏进出口公司要求延迟发货。其要求延迟发货的邮件如下：

Dear Paul Lockwood,

The goods you ordered are ready for shipment for a long time, but your amendment has not been reached here up to now. Today we contacted the shipping company and regret to tell you that we are unable to comply with your request. We have been informed that there is no available space on ships sailing from here to your port in October.

We are very sorry that we are unable to make the shipment as stipulated. So we have to ship the goods in November. Please amend the L/C, extending the date of shipment and validity to November 30 and December 15 respectively.

Yours Faithfully,
Shanghai Huaxia Imp. & Exp. Corp.
Michael Li
Sales Manager

请根据上述背景资料，以加拿大 James Brown & Sons 公司的名义给上海华夏进出口公司以回复，希望能够尽早发货，如能在 10 月发货，同意在香港转船。

11. Draft an e-mail advising Woolworth Co., Ltd., Melbourne, Australia to insure the goods they ordered, 10 000 dozen Towels, S/C No. 1108/80, which have been shipped per S.S. “Yellow River”, sailing on August 4, 2009.

1.3 Textiles Export Transactions

Business Background:

浙江金朝纺织有限公司主要生产牛仔布料，与巴拉圭 ABC 制衣厂（ABC Garment Factory）已有多次成功的贸易往来。最近一次订单完成后，客户发来投诉函，对牛仔布发货数量表示不满。该公司业务员说明理由，以积极的态度圆满处理投诉事情。

Business Requirements:

1. 熟悉公司情况和纺织品信息，尤其是牛仔布。
2. 能够根据订单要求起草合同。
3. 能够落实预付款，托收余款。
4. 熟悉装运通知的主要内容，能够根据要求撰写装运通知。
5. 能够针对客户的投诉函，撰写投诉处理函电。

Teaching Objective:

通过独立处理外贸业务中出现的各种问题，培养学生熟练开展外贸业务的能力。

Company Profile

Zhejiang Jinchao Textile Co., Ltd. is located in China's Orchid Village—Lanxi in the central and western part of Zhejiang Province. With the Hang-Jin-Qu Expressway, No. 330 National Road, Zhejiang-Jiangxi Railway Extension, Jin-Qian Railway and three rivers going through the city, Lanxi enjoys a reputation as "the confluence of three rivers, with convenient transportation access to seven provinces". Therefore, with our superior geographical position, we have a developed and convenient location.

With a total area of about 20 000 square meters, our company owns 70 jean-specialized rapier looms, a set of sizing-dying joint unit with frequency auto control system, and related equipment for the joint unit, including warping equipment, cloth plaiting machines, finishing machines and examination machines. Our company mainly produces products in six series, including pure cotton, polyester-mixed cotton and stretched jacquard, with a total of more than 500 types. We have more than 100 employees, producing over 3 million meters of all types of jeans annually.

The use of high-quality raw materials, comprehensive and efficient management, international standard production technology and a strict examination system, as well as our long-term accumulation of experience in production jointly ensure the quality of our products.

"Quality priority, honest cooperation and mutual benefit" have always been the core purpose of our company since the establishment. With the principle of "quality assurance, sincere service, mutual benefit and common development", we have won favorable comments from all clients. We sincerely welcome new and old customers to forward inquiries and cooperate with us.

Task 1 Drafting a Contract

Writing Background

浙江金朝纺织有限公司已经与巴拉圭 ABC 制衣厂完成了多次交易，最近该客户又给金朝纺织有限公司下来了订单。

Dear Zhang,

How are you? We are sorry to make your side wait so long.

At this moment, please send us the following order contract:

B40 (Article No.)-66"/67", 100% Cotton, 55 000 Meters, USD 2.90/M CIF ASUNCION.

Please don't forget the following instructions:

1) USD 2.90/M CIF price with shipping company HAMBURG SUD;

2) 100% Cotton;

3) 66"/67"Width;

4）30% First T/T and 70% balance payment by D/P at sight;

5）In total rolls, 85% up to 60 meters and 15% up to 30~60 meters;

6）All rolls with COMPUTER sticker information about meters roll No., quality grade, item number, composition, with importer's name.

Please send us the bank information for first T/T as well.

I am waiting for your contract and your bank information.

Best Regards,

John

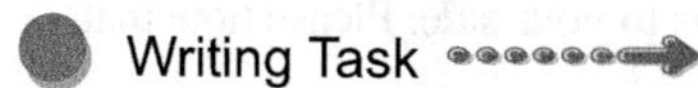

Writing Task

请以浙江金朝纺织有限公司业务员张敏（Amy Zhang）的名义写一封邮件：我公司得到巴拉圭方面的订单后，非常高兴，附上销售合同及相关文本。

Reference E-mail

Dear John,

Thanks for your kind reply and your understanding.

Please see the attached contract and bank information for you. Please check if they are OK. We are now waiting for your first T/T. Once we receive the first T/T, we will start the order production immediately.

Thanks again!

Best Regards,

Amy Zhang

Zhejiang Jinchao Textile Co., Ltd.

Task 2　Committing Advance Payment

Writing Background

巴拉圭 ABC Garment Factory 已支付第一笔 T/T 款项，特去函告知浙江金朝纺织有限公司，并附上付款凭证，希望对方在收到款项后亦向其通告。

Dear Zhang,

Today we have made the first T/T payment to your side. Attachment is the T/T swift copy, please check it. I think your side will receive the money quite soon. Once you receive the money, please let me know so that I can arrange our order at once.

Thanks very much!

Best Regards,

John

Writing Task

请以浙江金朝纺织有限公司业务员张敏（Amy Zhang）的名义写一封邮件，告知已收到巴拉圭 ABC Garment Factory 第一笔 T/T 款项，现正安排生产，承诺 40 天后备齐货物并发运。

Reference E-mail：

Dear John,

Hi! Today we received the first T/T from your side, so we will arrange the production at once. Around 40 days we will finish the total order quantity and ship the goods to your side. Please note that.

Thanks so much!

Best Regards,
Amy Zhang
Zhejiang Jinchao Textile Co., Ltd.

Task 3 Sending Shipping Advice

Writing Background

巴拉圭 ABC Garment Factory 的 John 给金朝纺织有限公司张敏发来邮件，要求其尽快发货。

Dear Zhang,

Hi, have your side finished my goods and arranged the shipment yet? I can’t wait any more for the goods as I have garment production plans urgently.

Please send us information about the delivery date and also send me the B/L[1]copy as soon as possible.

Thanks!

Best Regards,
John

Writing task

请给巴拉圭 ABC Garment Factory 的 John 写一封邮件，邮件包含下列内容：

1）货物的装运信息。

2）要求 ABC Garment Factory 准备余款。

3）金朝纺织有限公司将把整套装运单据交给银行办理托收。

Reference E-mail

Dear John,

How are you? Thanks for your E-mail.

We already shipped the goods on July 9, 2012. The following is the relavant shipping information:

Invoice No.:2012JC103

Quantity: 51 892 Meters

B/L No. : SEDU86110822

Port of Shipment : SHANGHAI

Port of Destination: ASUNCION

Ocean Vessel: SKY V.047A

Container/Seal Number: HMCU296264/JDRF254

We are glad to inform you that we have finished your order as contracted. We trust the goods will reach you in time for the selling season and prove to be entirely satisfactory. Please prepare your balance money, we'll present all shipping document to our bank for collection. Thank for your coopration.

Best Regards,

Amy Zhang

Zhejiang Jinchao Textile Co., Ltd.

Task 4 Complaints and Adjustments

Writing Background

装运通知发出后，浙江金朝纺织有限公司收到巴拉圭 ABC Garment Factory 的投诉邮件，投诉发货的数量没有达到订单要求，邮件内容如下：

Dear Zhang,

RE： YX-QS1306

We have received the shipping advice but we have a situation here. The buyer makes his final cost based on your information of stuffing, so in this case the buyer calculated the cost by 55 000Mts. But now after checking the shipping advice, we realized that you only shipped 51 800Mts, so the buyer is now having a difference on this container which he must cover by from his own pocket. The buyer is really mad and he's saying that if the container is not shipped, then we must load the container with 55 000Mts so we can cover the loses. Otherwise, he's refusing to receive the container. Please check by your side if there's anyway to fill the container and reach 55 000Mts, otherwise WE must take cover of the difference. Please check in your side how to do. Wait for your reply .

Best Regards,

John

Writing Task

请根据上述邮件，以浙江金朝纺织有限公司的名义给巴拉圭公司复函，内容包括：表达歉意，说明数量少的原因，并指出发货数量符合溢短装条款要求，希望对方理解。

Writing Guide

在买卖合同的履行过程中，经常会遇到各种各样的问题，尤其是当买方收到货物时，通常会以货物受损、货物缺失、货物错发等为由，提出索赔。在实际业务中，当一方提出索赔时，另一方首先要自查有没有过失。如有过失，应立即道歉，表示遗憾，并提出解决问题的建议；如对方无理索赔，应礼貌地拒绝。总之，对所有要求索赔的函电都要认真对待，并给予详细答复。

当出现贸易争端时，一般建议通过双方友好协商解决；协商不成的，可以提交仲裁。涉外经济仲裁是指涉外经济仲裁机构根据双方当事人在合同中订立的仲裁条款或者事后签订的仲裁协议，依法对涉外经济纠纷在事实上作出判断、在权利义务上作出裁决的法律制度。

涉外仲裁遵循协议、公平、独立裁决、保密审理和参照国际惯例的原则。

各国在长期的商业交往中已形成若干惯例，这些惯例既涉及实体法又涉及程序法。涉外仲裁机构在仲裁时，参照这些国际惯例可以弥补所在国法律法规的某些缺陷，也利于双方当事人接受裁决结果，从而合理、迅速地解决当事人之间的争执。

我国国际经济贸易仲裁委员会（原名对外经济贸易仲裁委员会），成立于 1956 年。我国国际经济贸易仲裁委员会由主任一人、副主任和委员若干人组成。按照《中国国际经济贸易仲裁委员会仲裁规则》的相关规定，我国国际经济贸易仲裁委员会主要管辖中外当事人之间、外国当事人之间和中国当事人之间产生的国际或涉外的契约性或非契约性的经济贸易等争议，例如合资经营、合作经营、合作开发、合作生产、技术转让、金融信贷、财产租赁、融资租赁、货物买卖、运输、保险、支付，以及来料加工、来件装配、补偿贸易等方面的案件。

There are two kinds of complaints being frequently made by buyers:

1）The genuine complaint, which arises from one of the following situations:①The wrong goods may have been sent; ②The quality may not be satisfactory; ③The goods may have been delivered damaged or late; ④The prices charged may be excessive, or not as agreed.

2）There is the complaint made by buyers who find fault with the goods as an excuse to escape from their contracts, either because they no longer want the goods or because they have found that they can get them cheaper elsewhere.

Therefore, as a seller, if you received a complaint, you should investigate the relevant issues in detail, and then considers how to deal with it.

When making a complaint, your E-mail should include the following points:

1）Begin by regretting the need to complaints;

2）Mention the number of the order, the date of shipment and the goods complained about;

3）State your reasons for being dissatisfied and ask for an explanation;

4) Refer to the inconvenience caused;

5) Suggest how the matter should be put right.

Replies to complaints should be courteous. If you are the seller, the following rules are to be noted when dealing with a complaint:

1) The first thing that has to be decided is whether the complaint is justified. If so, then you have to admit it readily, express your regret and promise to put matters right.

2) If the complaint is not justified, point this out politely and in an agreeable manner. It would be a wrong policy to refuse the claim offhand.

3) If you cannot deal with a complaint promptly, acknowledge it at once. Explain that you are looking into it and that you will send a full reply later.

4) All complaints should be treated as serious matters and thoroughly investigated.

Reference E-mail

Dear John,

Hi, thanks for your email.

Anyhow, we are sorry for this situation. We understand that the buyer makes his final cost based on the stuffing information, the more quantity we load the better it is for the buyer. But please note that the quantity we delivered is within the range allowed by the more or less clause in contract.

As you know, we make the production as per your order quantity. When the production is finished, we have about 55 000 meters totally actually. The reason why we send you 51 892 meters is that we are keeping the defective fabric to ourselves. We do not want to cheat you and mix the bad roll in the shipment, as you already asked us pay more attention to the fabric quality because of the order QS1305 before. If we just shrug off and load all the bad fabric, I think that is more terrible. That will bring much more serious consequence. Hope you can understand.

Best Regards,

Amy Zhang

Zhejiang Jinchao Textile Co., Ltd.

Task 5 Collecting the Balance

Writing Background

巴拉圭 ABC Garment Factory 在收到金朝纺织有限公司上述邮件后，表示理解，承诺将凭单托收余款，并且已经安排好款项，邮件如下：

Dear Zhang,

Study Situation 1

Thank you for your reply. We understand your stiuation.

We have arranged the balance payment. Please present the ready documents to the bank for collection immediately.

Thanks so much!

Best Regards,

John

Writing Task

请代浙江金朝纺织有限公司写一封邮件，告诉巴拉圭公司已经收到余款，并希望有机会再次合作。

Reference E-mails

Dear John,

We have got the balance money from the bank, thank you!

We are happy to finish your order smoothly and hope to cooprate again soon.

Best Regards,

Amy Zhang

Zhejiang Jinchao Textile Co., Ltd.

Specimen E-mails

(1) Order 1

Dear Lin:

The price quotes contained in your E-mail of May 4, 2013 gained favorable attention with us.

We would like to order the following shirts consisting of various colors, patterns and assortments:

Large 50 000pcs

Medium 40 000pcs

Small 30 000pcs

As the selling season is approaching, the total order quantity should be shipped in June. At that time an irrevocable L/C for the total value will be opened.

Please confirm the order and e-mail a shipping schedule.

Sincerely,

Tom

(2) Order 2

Dear Jenny,

We thank you for your Order No.568 received this morning for 10 000 dozen cotton shirts, but regret to have to disappoint you.

At present we have no stock of shirts in the size required and do not expect further shipment for at least another five weeks. Before then you may have been to obtain the shirts elsewhere, but if not we will notify you immediately our new stocks come in.

Yours Faithfully,
Ma Lin

(3) Acceptance 1

Dear Mr. Smith,

We thank you for your e-mail of Aug. 12, together with your orders G.697 and G.698. G.697 has been added to your Christmas order and G.698 is being made ready for immediate dispatch. We regret that we are still unable to supply "Wonderful" champagne glasses, but we are sending you "Nice", the alternative marked on your order.

We were very happy to learn of the success you are having with our glassware, and we shall be pleased to discuss with you for more favourable terms. When our representative, Mr. Zhang, calls on you in the next year, he will make you a better offer.

We send you our warmest congratulations on your increased business with us and look forward to further increases to our mutual benefit.

Yours Faithfully,
Zhang Lin

(4) Acceptance 2

Dear Mr. Jonson,

We are pleased to receive your order No. SY2013010 for shoes. We accept the order and are encolsing our Sales Contract No.589 in duplicate, please sign S/C and return one copy to us for our file.We ask you to open the relative L/C as soon as possible, so that we can ship the goods on time.

We are sure the goods will be proved to your satisfaction.

Yours faithfully,
Zhao Min

(5) Shipment 1

Dear Lily,

Re: S/C No. 698 Covering 5000 Cartons of Toilet Soap

We have received your E-mail yesterday in connection with the above subject.

In reply, we have the pleasure of informing you that the relevant L/C has been opened this morning. Upon receipt of the L/C, please arrange shipment of the goods booked by us without delay. We are informed by the local shipping company that S.S. "Brown" is due to sail from your city to our port on or about 15th October and, if possible, please try your best to ship by that steamer.

Should this trial order prove satisfactory to our customers, we can assure you that we shall place further larger orders with you in the near future.

Looking forward to your shipping advice soon.

Yours Faithfully,
Tom

(6) Shipment 2

Dear Aimee,

We refer to our Contract No. 897 which should be near the completion by this time. Due to a strike at Oakland port, which shows no sign of letting up for some time, we ask you to change the port of destination.

Would you please consign the goods to Seattle with no alteration in shipping date? Please confirm that you can carry out these new instructions.

Yours Faithfully,
Tony

(7) Shipment 3

Dear Jane,

We are pleased to inform you that your products under order No.689 were shipped on 21st , July 2013 per "COSCO SHANGHAI V.006W". Please find the details as follows:

Invoice No.: Jh2013015
Name of Vessel: COSCO SHANGHAI V.006W
CN/SN: GATU2032587/A80222
E.T.D.: 21st , July 2013
E.T.A.: 01st , AUG 2013
B/L NO.: COSU2013006
Shipping Company: COSCO Shipping Company
Freight Prepaid

We hope the goods will reach you at the due time. Meanwhile we are enclosing the copies of shipping documents.

Best Regards,
Li Lin

(8) Shipment 4

Dear John,

We are writing to you to notify that 3000 dozens of Shirts will be on board S.S[3] "Eastwind" sailing for London on 1st June. Kindly request you to insure the goods at once.

We are looking forward to your response as soon as possible.

Thank you very much.

Yours Faithfully,

Mingming

(9) Payment 1

Dear John,

Thank you for your e-mail of April 8 asking for a change in payment terms. As to new customer, we uasually accept payment by sight L/C. So I regret to say that we must insist on our usual practice and hope that you can understand us. We will inform you as soon as the goods are available.

Yours Faithfully,

Li Hua

(10) Payment 2

Dear Polly,

In the past, our purchases of steel pipes from you have normally been paid by confirmed, irrevocable letter of credit.

This arrangement has cost us a great deal of money. From the moment we open the credit until our buyers pay us normally ties up funds for about four months. This is currently a particularly serious problem for us in view of the difficult economic climate and the prevailing high interest rates.

If you could offer us easier payment terms, it would probably lead to an increase in business between our companies. We propose either cash against documents on arrival of goods, or drawing on us at three months' sight.

We hope our request will meet with your agreement and look forward to your early reply.

Yours Faithfully,

Abby

(11) Payment 3

Dear Bob,

We are the largest supermarket in India and have recently received a number of enquiries for your bicycles. We think there are good prospects for the sale of this product, but at present it is little known here and as we cannot count on regular sales we do not feel able to make purchases at our own expenses.

We are therefore writing to suggest that you send us a trial delivery for sale on D/A terms.

We make the proposal hoping to place firm orders when the market is established.

We believe our proposal offers good business opportunities and hope you will be willing to accept.

Yours Sincerely,
Lobin

(12) Claims 1

Dear Larry,

Our Order No.4312

We duly received the documents and took delivery of the goods on arrival of the S.S. "Isabella" at Hamburg.

We are much obliged to you for the prompt execution of this order. Everything appears to be correct and in good condition except in Case No. 71.

Unfortunately, when we opened this case we found it contained completely different articles, and we can only presume that a mistake was made and the contents of this case were for another order.

As we need the articles we ordered to complete deliveries to our customers, we must ask you to arrange for the dispatch of replacements at once. We attach a list of the contents of Case No. 71, and shall be glad if you will check this with our order and the copy of your invoice.

In the meantime, we are holding the above-mentioned case at your disposal. Please let us know what you wish us to do with it.

Yours Sincerely,
Jones

(13) Claims 2

Dear Jones,

Your Order No. 4312 per S.S. "Isabella"

Thank you for your E-mail of February 10 informing us that the consignment was delivered promptly. We appreciated your straightforwardness in pointing out that Case No. 71 did not contain the goods you ordered.

On going into the matter we find that a mistake was indeed made in the packing through a confusion of numbers, and we have arranged for the right goods to be dispatched to you at once. Relative documents will be mailed as soon as they are ready.

Please keep Case No. 71 and its contents until called for by our Commercial Counselor's Office, whom we have informed of the matter accordingly.

We were sorry for the trouble caused to you by the error and wish to assure you that care will be taken in the execution of your further orders.

Yours Sincerely,
Larry Huang

(14) Claims 3

Dear Mr. Robin,

Order NO. HT-2763

Thank you for your E-mail of 24 March. We are extremely sorry to learn that a mistake was made in Carton No.10 of the above order.

The missing 10 000 pens were sent this morning by Singapore Airways and the documents have already been forwarded to you.

We greatly regret the inconvenience caused by this and offer our sincere apologies. We can assure you that every effort will be made to ensure that similar errors do not occur again.

Best Wishes,

Jessica Hua

(15) Claims 4

Dear Tom,

I appreciate your prompt reply.

After studying your reply to our complaint, we are sorry to tell you that we can not agree with you. We insist that you are held liable for it completely. If no settlement can be reached, the case in dispute shall then be submitted for arbitration in our country.

We hope you will make a prompt decision.

Thanks and regards!

John

(16) Claims 5

Dear John,

Thank you for your e-mail.

After clear consideration and investigation, we also insist that the damage doesn't rest with us completely which is stated clearly in Certificate of Survey. Considering our long-term cooperation, we would like to settle the claim through negotiation. If you insist your proposal, we will accept the reward of arbitration.

Rgds.

Tom

(17) Claims 6

Dear Jane,

From last shipment we have problems with top lights —see pictures. They are broken. We would have thought the damage may be due to the shipping company. We claimed on them for recovery of the loss, but an investigation made by the surveyor has revealed the fact that the damage is attributable to improper packing.

We did not have this problem before, so TALK to your supplyer about it —I had to take out of new product and change it. It cost me a lot because my crew have to do it and it is all over Belgium. I think I should get some disscount for fixing this.

Hope you will be able to solve all my problems so that I don't have to spend much time talking to angry clients.

And hope your next container will be OK. MAKE SURE YOU CHECK IT BEFORE SENDING!!! I have toooooo many problems, especially my competitors have the same product —so I cannot afford to have so many problems with MY PRODUCT!!!

Listen, each case cost me a lot —what do we do with that???

P.S. We claim on you to compensate us for the loss, $700, which we have sustained by the damage to the goods.

Thanks and regards.

John

(18) Claims 7

Dear John,

Thanks very much for your E-mail! We have studied your surveyor's report very carefully.

The goods have been packed as you requested. I think it may be damaged when being handled at the container yard or on the port of transshipment. We are therefore not responsible for the damage. However, as we do not think that it would be fair to have you bear the loss alone, we suggest that the loss be divided between both of us, to which we hope you will agree. Let me know your answers.

Rgds.

Jane

Notes

1. B/L：Bill of Lading（提单）是由船长或承运人或承运人的代理人签发的，证明收到特定货物，允许将货物运至特定目的地并交付于收货人的凭证。提单的作用有三点：一是运输合同的证明，二是货物收据，三是物权凭证。

提单可按照下列五种方式进行分类：

1）按货物是否已装船分类，分为已装船提单（Shipped B/L or on Board B/L）和收货待运提单（Received for Shipment B/L）。

2）按提单抬头分类，分为记名提单（Straight B/L），又称收货人抬头提单，指示提单（Order B/L）和不记名提单（Blank B/L or Open B/L）。

3）按有无批注分类，分为清洁提单（Clean B/L）和不清洁提单（Foul B/L）。

4）按收费方式分类，分为运费预付提单（Freight Prepaid B/L）和运费到付提单（Freight Collect B/L）。

5）按船舶的经营方式分类，分为班轮提单（Liner B/L）和租船提单（Charter Parth B/L）。

2. COSCO：中国远洋运输（集团）总公司（China Ocean Shipping(Group) Company）。COSCO 是中国大陆最大的航运企业，全球最大的海洋运输公司之一，中华人民共和国 53 家由中央直管的特大型国企之一。1961 年 4 月 27 日成立中国远洋运输公司（交通部远洋运输局），1993 年 2 月 16 日组建以中国远洋运输（集团）总公司为核心企业的中国远洋运输集团。

3. S.S：steamship（船运），一般用在船名前。

Important Words and Phrases

1. cloth plaiting machine	码布机
2. commercial invoice	商业发票
3. in one's favor/ in favor of sb.	以某人为受益人（抬头人）
4. irrevocable L/C	不可撤销信用证
5. jacquard	提花织物
6. jean-specialized rapier looms	牛仔专用剑杆织机
7. open account terms（O/A terms）	赊账方式
8. sizing-dying joint unit with frequency auto control system	变频自控系统浆染联合机
9. standing	永久的，固定的；地位，身份，状况
e.g.standing order	常年的订单
credit/financial standing	信用/财务状况
10. stretched	弹力
11. warping	整经
12. polyester-mixed cotton	涤棉面料
13. pure cotton	纯棉
14. survey report	检验报告
15. This is to certify…	兹证明……
16. to be ready for desparch	准备发货
17. to compensate for	赔偿
18. to hold sb. responsible for sth.	要某人负责某事
19. to lodge/file/put in a claim against/with sb.	对某人提出索赔
20. to offset the difference	抵消差额
21. to submit an insurance claim / lodge a claim	提出保险索赔
22. sample	样品
23. representative sample	代表性样品
24. fair avarge quality（FAQ）	大路货（良好平均品质）
25. original sample	原样
26. duplicate sample	复样
27. countersample	对等样品
28. reference sample	参考样品

29. sealed sample 封样
30. tolerance 公差
31. assortment 花色（搭配）
32. 5% more or less 5%增减
33. ocean bill of lading 海运提单
34. air way bill 空运提单
35. packing list 装箱单
36. shipping order 装货单
37. insurance policy 保险单
38. claim 索赔
39. penalty 罚金条款
40. force Majeure 不可抗力
41. certificate of origin 原产地证明书
42. inspection certificate of quanlity 品质检验证书
43. inspection certificate of weight 重量检验证书
44. Commodity Inspection Bureau (C.B.I.) 商品检验局
45. inspection certificate 检验证书
46. disputes 争议
47. arbitration 仲裁
48. arbitral tribunal 仲裁庭

Useful Expressions

1. If your prices are favorable, we can place an order with you at once.
2. We'd like to know what you can offer as well as your sales conditions.
3. Could you tell me which kind of payment terms you'll choose?
4. Will you please tell us the earliest possible date you can make shipment?
5. Do you take special orders?
6. We can't accept your offer unless the price is reduced by 5%.
7. You'll see that our offer compares favorably with the quotations you can get elsewhere.
8. We have extended the offer as per your request.
9. All prices in the price lists are subject to our confirmation.
10. Business is closed at this price.
11. We regret we have to maintain our original price.
12. We've already cut the price very fine.
13. The utmost (best) we can do is to reduce the price by 2%.
14. Nothing wrong will happen, so long as the quality of your article is good.
15. If the quality of your products is satisfactory, we may place regular orders.
16. We sincerely hope the quality are in conformity with the contract stipulations.

17. We always have faith in the quality of your products.

18. A shortage of 50M/Ts is a big loss for us.

19. Have you seen the shortage claim from our company?

20. Please make an offer indicating the packing.

21. We've informed the manufacturer to have them packed as per your instruction.

22. I'm sure the new packing will give your clients satisfaction.

23. Normally, packing charge is included in the contract price.

24. We have especially reinforced out pacing in order to minimize the extent of any possible damage to the goods.

25. The goods are to be packed in strong export cases, securely strapped.

26. In case one party fails to carry out the contract, the other party is entitled to cancel the contract.

27. We can't accept any other terms of payment.

28. We've drawn a clean draft on you for the value of this sample shipment.

29. As an integral part of the contract, the inspection of goods has its special importance.

30. We'll accept the goods only if the results from the two inspections are identical with each other.

31. What if the results from the inspection and the reinspection do not coincide with each other?

32. Our Inspection Bureau will issue a Veterinary Inspection Certificate to show that the shipment is in conformity with export standards.

33. The underwriters are responsible for the claim as far as it is within the scope of cover.

34. The extent of insurance is stipulated in the basic policy form and in the various risk clause.

35. The insurance rate for such kink of risk will vary according to the kind.

36. W.P.A coverage is too narrow for a shipment of this nature, please extend the coverage to include TPND.

37. I'm sorry to tell you that we are unable to give you a definite date of shipment for the time being.

38. We'd better have a brief talk about the loading port.

39. We assure you that shipment will be made no later than the first half of April.

40. We sincerely hope that both quality and quantity are in conformity with the contract stipulations.

41. We are sorry to learn that your goods were badly damaged during transit and the insurance company will compensate you for the losses accordingly to the coverage arranged.

42. An insurance claim should be submitted to the insurance company or its agents within 30 days after the arrival of the consignment at the port of destination.

43. Should any damage be incurred, you may approach the insurance agents at your end and

submit an insurance claim supported by a survey report.

44. We have to hold you responsible for the loss we have been made to sustain.

45. As the goods are not identical with the L/C, we cannot help lodging a claim against you.

46. As you failed to make delivery in time, we have no choice but to cancel our order with you.

47. The goods under our Order No. 1236 should have reached us a week ago.

48. We were very sorry to receive your complaint that the material you received was not of the quality expected.

49. Your claim should be supported by sufficient evidence.

50. I hope you'll be entirely satisfied with this initial shipment.

Exercises

1. Write an e-mail advising Continental Trading Co., Ltd., 24th Street, Rangoon, that the shipping space of 20 000 bales of cotton, purchased on FOB basis from Sunny Trading Company, has been booked on S.S. "Yamata Maru", which is scheduled to call at Rangoon on 15th November.

2. An Italian buyer has ordered 600 cases of green tea from Hangzhou Imp. & Exp. Corp. upon arrival at Milan port, 80 cases were found completely wet. The Italian buyer lodges a claim against this. Please write an e-mail on behalf of the buyer to the above matter.

3. 某公司将进口一批家用电器，价格条款是 CFR，发货日期是 9 月。为了在发出货物之前能及时投保，要求出口方订好舱位后，立即发出装运通知，告之船名、航次、开船时间等，以便按时投保。请根据上述要求，代表进口方拟写一份函电。

4. Wirte an e-mail based on the following information:

你方给客户的袜子报价，客户 8 月 10 日邮件中认为价格偏高。请给客户回复邮件，内容包括：

1）最近原料价格上涨；

2）产品质量上乘；

3）客户需要数量只有 500 打，不能给数量折扣；

4）公司考虑近期调价，价格将有所上涨，请客户尽快回复。

5. Please write an e-mail according to the following points:

1）经过洽谈，各项条款已经谈妥，决定订购 10 000 台"华为"平板电脑。

2）"华为"产品市场声誉较好，质量优良，售后服务也好，因此，希望建立长期的合作关系。

3）希望早日收到销售合同。

Study Situation 1

1.1 Small Commodities Export Transaction

Business Background:

浙江欣欣饰品有限公司地处义乌市，成立于 1990 年，公司专业生产并出口银饰品。最近该公司收到美国老客户 Sun Trading Co., Ltd.的询盘，作为公司业务助理，你要协助业务员进行贸易磋商，签订合同，最终顺利完成出口业务。

Business Requirements:

1. 熟悉公司情况和饰品信息，尤其是时尚戒指。
2. 了解商务函电的格式、写作原则等。
3. 能够根据客户询盘撰写报盘函。
4. 能够根据订单起草合同，撰写签约函。
5. 能够落实预付款，撰写付款函。
6. 可以根据对方对包装的要求撰写包装函。
7. 会撰写装运函，并寄出装船单据。
8. 能够撰写业务善后函。

Teaching Objective:

通过协助有经验的业务员开展外贸业务，培养外贸业务的实际操作能力。

Company Profile

Zhejiang Xinxin Ornament Co., Ltd. established in 1990 and located in Yiwu City is a manufacturer and exporter of sterling silver fashion jewelry with designing and wholesaling. There are more than 500 employees, including 50 professional design staff. The products are being exported to clients in Europe, North America and Asia.

We specialize in 925 sterling silver jewelry, brass jewelry, and jewelry containing semi-precious stones, of which we have many years of experience on production and marketing. The main products include necklaces, bracelets, rings, earrings, toe rings, bangles, brooches and tie clips, currently offering over 15,000 styles.

The company can also do the international business on OEM[1] & ODM[2] basis. New product development, customer-oriented items, timely delivery and technical service are all handled by professionals. Prompt response will be guaranteed. With the principle of "Quality First", we

Task 1 Plan On Marketing

Writing Background

广东华夏化工有限公司想要找一个来料加工的合作伙伴开展来料加工业务。该合作伙伴能够提供皂基，回购加工出来的香皂。

Writing Task

请为广东华夏化工有限公司起草一份来料加工客户开拓计划。

Writing Guide

来料加工是指进口料件由境外企业提供、经营企业不需要付汇进口，按照境外企业的要求进行加工或者装配，只收取加工费，制成品由境外企业销售的经营活动。来料加工方式下，进口料件和出口成品的所有权都归外商所有，承接来料加工的出口企业只收取加工费，没有定价权。

来料加工方式下，海关对企业进口的原材料或零部件等予以保税，加工产品出口时，海关对出口货物及企业收取的加工费收入免征出口环节的关税、增值税等，但出口货物所耗用国内辅件所支付的进项税额不得抵扣或不予退税。

来料加工的操作流程一般如下：①签订来料加工合同；②外贸主管部门备案；③海关申领加工贸易手册；④进口原材料或零部件；⑤组织加工或装配；⑥报检报关出口；⑦合同核销结案。

在来料加工贸易方式中，国外客户选择首先要考虑的是料件的供应能力，以及成品的回购能力。本案例中，需要寻找能够提供皂基，回购香皂的国外客户。皂基一般由牛羊油、椰子油和棕榈油等加工而成，澳大利亚、新西兰牛羊油、椰子油出口较多，马来西亚、印度尼西亚等东南亚国家盛产椰子油、棕榈油。在考虑来料加工合作伙伴的选择上，可以优先考虑这些地区。

Reference Plan

Plan on Marketing

In order to find out a suitable business partner and carry out the business on processing with supplied materials, we make a plan as follows :

Materials and Finished Products : Soap Base[2], Toilet Soap

Ability of Business Partner : Ability on supply of soap base and purchase of toilet soap.

Target Country : Australia, Newzeland, Malaysia, Indonesia.

Channels : Old customers, new customers from Fairs and Internet

Responsible Person : Lin Nan from Marketing, and Li feng as her assistant

Task 2 Negotiation

Writing Background

澳大利亚 Cardle Australia Limited 发来邮件，表示希望提供皂基给广州华夏化工有限公司用于生产香皂，然后回购香皂，支付加工费。具体邮件如下：

Dear Miss Lin,

We have done business for many years and are satisfied with the quality of your toilet soap. Considering having a large quantity of tallow oil in Australia, we wish to do processing trade with you. That's to say, we supply you with soap base, you process them into toilet soaps for us, we pay you processing fees. Is it OK?

Waiting for your good news!

Best Regards,
Peter

Writing Task

请代表广东华夏化工有限公司回复澳大利亚 Cardle Australia Limited 公司，邮件包含下列内容：

1）对他们提出的来料加工建议很感兴趣；

2）希望澳大利亚公司派人来中国进行来料加工贸易磋商。

Reference E-mail

Dear Peter,

Thank you for your e-mail dated Aug. 20, 2013.

We are interested in your suggestion. Tell you the truth, your desire to do business on processing trade with us coincides with ours. Could you send somebody to China for the details of processing trade?

Best Regards,
Lin Nan

Task 3 Drafting Contract

Writing Background

澳大利亚 Cardle Australia Limited 公司的 Peter 前来广东华夏化工有限公司，双方就加工贸易合同条款细节进行谈判并签订合同。

Writing Task

请根据谈判结果，起草来料加工合同。

Writing Guide

来料加工合同必须包含加工商品的名称和数量、加工费用、损耗率、支付方式等主要内容。合同样本如下。

来料加工合同

订约人：×××有限公司（以下简称甲方）

×××有限公司（以下简称乙方）

兹经双方同意，甲方委托乙方在________加工×××，一切所需的原料由甲方提供，其条款如下：

1. 来料加工的商品和数量

（1）商品名称——×××。

（2）数量——共计_______。

2. 一切所需用的原料由甲方提供，或乙方在____________或___________购买，清单附于本合同内。

3. 加工费如下：USD ×××（大写：____美元）。

4. 加工所需的主要原料由甲方运至_______，若有短少或破损，甲方应负责补充供应。

5. 甲方应于成品交运前一个月，开立信用证或电汇全部加工费用及由乙方在__________或_________购买的原料费用。

6. 乙方应在双方同意的时间内完成×××的加工和交运，不得延迟，凡发生无法控制的和不可预见的情况例外。

7. 原料的损耗率：加工时原料损耗率为_____%，其损耗率由甲方免费供应，如损耗率超过____%，应由乙方补充加工所需之原料。

8. 若甲方误运原料，或因大意而将原料超运，乙方应将超运部分退回，其费用由甲方承担，若遇有短缺，应由甲方补充。

9. 甲方提供加工×××原料，乙方应严格按规定的要求加工，不得变更。

10. 与本合同有关的一切进出口手续应由乙方予以办理。

11. 加工后的×××，乙方应运交给甲方随时指定的国外买方。

12. 其他条件

（1）×××的商标应由甲方提供，若出现法律纠纷，甲方应负完全责任。

（2）为促进出口业务，乙方应储备样品，随时可寄往甲方所指定的国外买主，所需的原料从甲方所运来的原料中扣除。

13. 本合同一式三份，甲方与乙方在签字后各执一份，另一份呈送__________有关部门备案。

×××有限公司 ________ ×××有限公司________

经理 经理

Reference Contract

CONTRACT FOR PROCESSING WITH SUPPLIED MATERIALS

Cardle Australia Limited (hereinafter called Party A) and Guangdong Huaxia Chemical Co., Ltd. (hereinafter called Party B) have agreed that Party B shall manufacture Toilet Soap in Guangdong with all necessary materials supplied by Party A under the following terms and conditions:

1. Commodity and quantities for processing with supplied materials:

(1) Commodity: Toilet Soap ;

(2) Quantity: 600 tons in total.

2. All necessary materials listed in the contract shall be supplied by Party A.

3. The processing charge is at USD 500 000 (SAY: US Dollars Five Hundred Thousand Only) and the packing charge is 400 000 (SAY: US Dollars Four Hundred Thousand Only).

4. The main materials required for processing will be sent to Guangzhou by Party A and if there is any shortage or damage, Party A should be held responsible for supplying replacements.

5. Party A should pay Party B by L/C covering the full amount of processing charges and packing charges one month before shipment of the finished products.

6. Party B must complete the manufacturing of all toilet soaps and effect shipment within the agreed date without delay except in the occurrence of uncontrollable and unforceeable events.

7. The damage rate[3] of materials: The damage rate of materials in processing is 10 % and such a damage rate of materials shall be supplied free by Party A, should the damage rate exceed 10 % , Party B shall supply additional materials.

8. Should shipment of materials sent by Party A be wrong or in excess, Party B shall return the excessive portion at the expense of Party A, in case of short shipment, Party A shall make up the shortage.

9. All materials supplied by Party A for Toilet Soap shall be processed by Party B strictly in accordance with the requirements without any modification.

10. All import and export formalities in connection with this contract should be handled by Party B.

11. All Toilet Soap processed by Party B shall be shipped to the foreign buyers appointed by Party A at anytime.

12. Other terms and conditions:

(1) The trade marks[4] of Toilet Soap shall be supplied by Party A, should there be any legal dispute, Party A shall be held fully responsible;

(2) For promotional purposes, Party B shall prepare samples of Toilet Soap at any time and send them to foreign Buyers appointed by Party A, all materials required would be supplied out of the stock supplied by Party A;

13. This contract shall be made in triplicate, Party A and Party B shall, both signing all copies, retain one copy and submit one to authorities concerned in(place) for registration.

Cardle Australia Limited	Guangdong Huaxia Chemical Co., Ltd
____________	____________
Manager	Manager

Notes

1. Sales Revenue: 产品销售或服务的收入。

2. Soap Base: 皂基。一般分为透明皂基和白色皂基。主要成分为牛羊油/椰子油/棕榈油、植物甘油、水、糖、山梨（糖）醇。透明皂基可制作透明精油皂、手工皂、美容洁面皂、造型皂、各类洗涤皂等；白色皂基可制作手工皂、混色纹理手工皂、美容皂、沐浴皂、造型皂及各类洗涤皂等。

3. Damage Rate: 损耗率。此处指皂基在加工成香皂的过程中，因意外或人为造成的损耗，其损耗量所占的总量的百分率。

4. Trade Mark: 商标。根据商标管理分类，可分为注册商标和未注册商标。经过商标注册的商标称为注册商标，即经使用商标人按照法定手续向国家商标局申请注册，经过审核后准予核准注册的商标。反之，则为未注册商标。

Important Words and Phrases

1. processing trade	加工贸易
2. processing with supplied materials	来料加工
3. assembling with supplied parts	来件装配
4. finished product	成品
5. direct selling	直销
6. sales representative	销售代表
7. the VAT reform	增值税改革
8. export tax rebates	出口退税
9. examing and approving	审核批准
10. the system of keeping records	备案制度
11. the export mix	出口商品结构
12. upgrading of processing trade	加工贸易升级
13. the processing charge	加工费

14. supplying replacements	补充供应
15. unforceeable events	不可预见的事件
16. prepare samples	储备样品
17. legal dispute	法律纠纷
18. in triplicate	一式三份
19. the cheap labor	低廉的劳动力
20. the world labor price	国际劳务价格
21. process in strict accordance with the design	严格按照设计加工
22. visible trade	有形贸易
23. invisible trade	无形贸易
24. barter trade	易货贸易
25. bilateral trade	双边贸易
26. triangle trade	三角贸易
27. multilateral trade	多边贸易
28. counter trade	对销贸易；抵偿贸易
29. counter purchase	互购贸易
30. buy-back	回购贸易

Useful Expressions

1. We are glad to know you wish to do processing trade with us.
2. I'm not sure if it would be convenient for you to visit our company next month.
3. We are looking forward to your coming for negotiation on processing trade.
4. It is win-win business for us if you can supply raw materials and we process them.
5. If you can process plastic tubes for us, please let me know.
6. We hope you can assemble the TV set for us and we would give you reasonable processing charges.
7. When you process the products, please accord to the samples we supplied.
8. All materials supplied by us will arrive Shanghai port before the end of October, don't be worry about it.
9. Your L/C covering the full amount of processing charges should be reached us one month before shipment of the finished products.
10. All materials supplied by Party A for the products shall be processed by Party B strictly in accordance with the Party A's requirements without any modification.
11. We'll improve the quality of our products and production efficiency.
12. We will process ASAP after we received the raw materials you send us.
13. We've received your sample for processing last Sunday.
14. Would you accept delivery spread over a period of time?

15. We have always been able to supply these firms with their monthly requirements without interruption.

16. We take this opportunity to re-emphasize that we shall, at all times, do everything possible to give you whatever information you desire.

17. We shall be very glad to cooperate with you at very reasonable processing charges.

18. If your quotations are suitable and the quality proves good，we'll be pleased to invite your representative over for detailed discussion.

19. If you want any changes, we can make minor alternations.

20. Is there any way of ensuring we'll have enough time for our talks?

Exercises

Traslate the following Chinese sentences into English.

1. 请按照来样进行加工。
2. 对电脑的装配要严格按照图纸及其说明进行。
3. 来料加工过程中，原料损耗率超过 10%的部分，费用由加工方承担。
4. 来料加工贸易方式下，进口原料和出口成品的所有权都属于外商。
5. 从事加工贸易的企业都必须到海关申领加工贸易手册。

2.2 Processing with Imported Materials

Business Background:

浙江嘉华管业有限公司专业生产各种管材管件，产品大多销往海外。为了降低原材料成本，提高出口产品竞争力，公司决定开展进料加工业务，进口塑料粒子，加工成铝塑复合管之后再出口。

Business Requirements:

1. 熟悉公司，了解塑料粒子和铝塑管材。
2. 能够进行进口询盘。
3. 能够运用函电进行进口洽谈，签订进口合同。
4. 能够填写开证申请书。
5. 了解进料加工操作流程。
6. 能够运用函电熟练开展进出口业务。

Teaching Objective:

让学生充分了解进料加工流程，培养学生运用函电独立开展进出口业务的能力。

Company Profile

Zhejiang Jiahua Tube Co., Ltd. was established in 1980, located in Hangzhou City, Zhejiang Province, which lies in the Yangtze River Delta Economic Circle, enjoys its exceptional regional superiority in developed logistics and transport facilitation as a key position. It only takes 15 minutes to Xiaoshan International Airport by car. The company covers an area of 50 000 square meters, including seven modern standard workshops and one comprehensive office building. It is a professional manufacturer and exporter of PAP(Pex-AL-Pex) pipe, Pipe PP-R, Compress Fittings, PVC pipe clamp, Press Fittings, Valves, Purifie, Tape, Water Meter and so on.

We pay much attention to the development of new products and transformation of scientific research achievements, and have kept a long-term cooperation with relative colleges and research institutes for exploitation and application of up-to-date materials. In an effort to introduce elements of high-quality and world competitive mechanism, we have been marching into overseas markets to win more shares in high-end products in the relevant field.

With powerful financial strength, advanced managerial concept, excellent marketing service, strict quality control system and the whole scientific method, we would like to develop together with you hand in hand. Adhering to the operation principle of "Faith First, Clients Uppermost", we will return you with high-quality products and complete after-sale service with the lowest price.

If you are interested in any of our products, please feel free to contact us for more details. You are welcome to visit our factory in Hangzhou, or to simply browse our website. We sincerely hope to establish long-term cooperation relationship with you on the basis of mutual benefit, reciprocity and common development!

Task 1 Inquiry

Writing Background

浙江嘉华管业有限公司想要进口塑料粒子，用于加工管材。公司业务员黄小丽（Lily Huang）在阿里巴巴网站看到印度尼西亚的 PT.DERO International 公司正在销售塑料粒子，于是便发去邮件进行询盘。

Writing Task

请为浙江嘉华管业有限公司业务员黄小丽（Lily Huang）撰写一封询盘函，内容包括信息来源、邮件目的等。

Writing Guide

进料加工贸易是指我方用外汇购买进口的原材料、辅料、零部件、元器件、配套件、包装物料等，经加工成成品或半成品后再外销出口的交易形式。进料加工贸易方式下，进口原材料的所有权和收益权属于经营企业。

进料加工的特点：

1）中方企业自行从国际市场组织原辅材料，进口时需对外付汇。

2）中方企业需自行开拓国际市场，寻找客户，接洽订单。

3）中方企业对从原辅料进口直至成品销售的全过程独立承担商业风险。

4）中方企业自行开展进口和出口两笔业务。

进料加工的流程：

1）登记备案。出口企业开展进料加工复出口业务，在向海关申请进口料件免税之前，必须先持经贸主管部门颁发的《加工贸易业务批准证》、《进口料件及出口成品申请备案清单》、《出口制成品及对应进口料件消耗备案清单》、和海关《进料加工登记手册》，送主管出口退税税务部门审核签章，税务部门须逐笔登记并将复印件留存备查。

2）出具证明。有进料加工业务的生产企业，在向退税部门申报办理“免、抵、退”税时应填报《生产企业加工进口料件申报明细表》，退税部门按规定审核后，出具《生产企业进料加工贸易免税证明》。

3）业务核销。生产企业《进料加工登记手册》最后一笔出口业务在海关核销之后，《进料加工登记手册》被海关收缴之前，持《进料加工登记手册》原件及《生产企业进料加工海关登记手册核销申请表》，到退税部门办理进料加工业务核销手续。退税部门根据进口料件和出口货物的实际发生情况出具《进料加工登记手册》核销后的《生产企业进料加工贸易免税证明》，与当期出具的《生产企业进料加工贸易免税证明》一并参与计算。

Reference E-mail

Dear Huma,

We have your name and address from http://www.alibaba.com and are happy to learn that you are selling plastic granule. As we want to purchase this item for processing and shall be very pleased to enter into trade relations with you.

Our company was founded in 1980, having more than 30 years of import and export experience. We specialize in PAP pipe, PP-R Pipe, Compress Fittings, PVC pipe clamp, Press Fittings, Valves, Purifie, Tape, Water Meter and so on. We are interested in your Plastic Granules. Would you please send us your favorable price for 600 tons?

We look forward to your early reply and hope that we shall be able to conclude some transactions with you in the near future.

Sincerely Yours,

Lily

Task 2 Acceptance

Writing Background

印度尼西亚 PT.DERO International 公司的 Huma 发来邮件，对塑料粒子进行了报价。具体邮件如下：

Dear Miss Lily,

In reply to your E-mail of March 20, 2013, we are making you the following offer:

Commodity: Plastic Granule

Model Number: PP[1] , LLDPE[2] , HDPE[3]

Place of Origin: Indonesia

Packing: In Plastic Bag , 40 ft Container[4] , Export Standard

Quantity: 600 tons.

Price: USD1000 per ton FOB Jakarta , Indonesia.

Shipment: One month after receipt of your L/C allowing transshipment and partial shipment.

Payment: By 100% confirmed irrevocable letter of credit in our favor available by draft at sight.

Thank you for your inquiry. We are looking forward to your good news.

Best Regards,

Huma

Writing Task

请代表浙江嘉华管业有限公司业务员黄小丽（Lily Huang）撰写一封邮件，回复印度尼西亚的 PT.DERO International 公司。邮件包含下列内容：

1）表示接受报盘。

2）希望印度尼西亚的 PT.DERO International 公司尽快起草销售合同。

Reference E-mail

Dear Huma,

Thank you for your offer for plastic granule.

Your offer is workable for us. Attached you could find the updated PO[5]. As this is the first transaction between us, we hope you can pay attention to it.

Best Regards,

Lily

Attachment:

PURCHASE ORDER

<table>
<tr><td colspan="2">SELLER</td><td colspan="3">BUYER</td></tr>
<tr><td colspan="2">PT.DERO INTERNATIONAL
SYAITAM NO.20, KAMPUNG KEDEP DESA TLAJUNG UDIK
KECAMATAN GUNUNG PUTRI
KABUPATEN BOGOR 15862
JAWA BARAT INDONESIA，15862</td><td colspan="3">ZHEJIANG JINHUA Tube Co., Ltd
ROOM 823, WULIN MANSION, WULIN ROAD, HANGZHOU, ZHEJIANG, P.R.CHINA</td></tr>
<tr><td colspan="5">SHIP VIA: FROM JAKARTA TO NINGBO BY SEA.</td></tr>
<tr><td>ITEMS</td><td>DESCRIPTION</td><td>QUANTITY</td><td>UNIT PRICE</td><td>TOTAL</td></tr>
<tr><td>Plastic Granule</td><td>PP
LLDPE
HDPE</td><td>200tons
200tons
200tons</td><td>FOB Jakarta
USD1000/ ton
USD1000/ ton
USD1000/ ton</td><td>200 000.00
200 000.00
200 000.00</td></tr>
<tr><td>NOTES:</td><td colspan="4">Other terms as your offer.</td></tr>
<tr><td>PO NO.</td><td>PT1315</td><td>Date:</td><td colspan="2">April 10,2013</td></tr>
</table>

Task 3　Signing the Contract

Writing Background

印度尼西亚 PT.DERO International 公司的 Huma 给浙江嘉华管业有限公司业务员黄小丽发来邮件，并通过快递寄来塑料粒子销售合同一式二份，要求嘉华公司会签，并返还一份供其存档。邮件内容如下：

Dear Lily,

Thanks for your PO. We are sending you our signed Sales Contract No.PT1310 in duplicate by DHL[6], please counter sign and return one copy to us for file. If there is any problems, please let me know without delay.

You may rest assured that your order will receive our best attention.

Best Regards,

Huma

Enclosure:

SALES CONTRACT

编号 S/C No.: PT1310
日期 Date: April 20, 2013
签约地点 Signed At: Jakarta, Indonesia

卖方 Sellers：PT.DERO INTERNATIONAL
SYAITAM NO.20, KAMPUNG KEDEP DESA TLAJUNG UDIK
KECAMATAN GUNUNG PUTRI
KABUPATEN BOGOR 15862
JAWA BARAT INDONESIA，15862

买方 Buyers：ZHEJIANG JINHUA Tube Co., Ltd
ROOM 823, WULIN MANSION, WULIN ROAD, HANGZHOU , ZHEJIANG, P.R.CHINA

兹买卖双方同意成交下列商品，双方订立条款如下：

The contract is made by and agreed between the buyer and the seller in accordance with the terms and conditions stupilated below:

1. 品名及规格 Name of Commodity and Specification	2. 数量 Quantity	3. 单价及价格条款 Unit Price	4. 金额 Amount USD	5. 总值 Total Value USD
Plastic Granule		FOB Jakarta		
PP	200tons	USD1000/ ton	200 000.00	600 000.00
LLDPE	200tons	USD1000/ ton	200 000.00	
HDPE	200tons	USD1000/ ton	200 000.00	

数量及总值均可有 10%的增减，由卖方决定。

With 10% more or less both in amount and quantity allowed at the Seller's option.

6. 包装 Packing：塑料袋包装，40 英尺普通货柜，符合出口标准。In Plastic Bag , 40 ft. Container , Export Standard.

7. 装运期限：☑ 收到信用证后一个月内发货，允许转运和分批装运。

Time of Shipment: ☑ One month after receipt of your L/C allowing transshipment and partial shipment.

8. 装运口岸：雅加达。

Port of Loading: Jakarta.

9. 目的港：宁波。

Port of Destination: Ningbo.

10. 付款条件：☑ 100%保兑的不可撤销的即期信用证付款，以卖方为受益人。

Terms of Payment: ☑ By 100% confirmed irrevocable letter of credit in our favor available by draft at sight.

11. 保险：☑ 由买方投保。

Insurance: ☑ To be covered by the buyer.

12. 装船标记 Shipping Marks: N/M.

13. 备注（REMARKS）

卖方	买方
THE SELLERS	THE BUYERS
PT.DERO INTERNATIONAL	ZHEJIANG JINHUA Tube Co., Ltd

Writing task

请回函告诉印度尼西亚公司，已经会签合同，并已用快递寄出，提请查收。

Reference E-mail:

Dear Huma,

Very glad to receive your S/C, thank you!

We have couter-signed the S/C and sent one copy to you by courier service, please check it.

Best Regards,

Lily

Task 4 Applying for Issuing an L/C

Writing Background

浙江嘉华管业有限公司和印度尼西亚的 PT.DERO International 公司已成功签下销售合同。根据合同规定，作为进口方的嘉华公司要通过银行开立相关的信用证。

Writing task

请根据 Sales Contract No.PT1310 的内容为浙江嘉华管业有限公司填写开证申请书。

Writing Guide

开证申请书的填写：

1）DATE（申请开证日期）。在申请书右上角填写实际申请日期。

2）TO（致）。银行印制的申请书上事先都会印就开证银行的名称、地址，银行的 SWIFT CODE、TELEX NO.等也可同时显示。

3）PLEASE ISSUE ON OUR BEHALF AND/OR FOR OUR ACCOUNT THE FOLLOWING IRREVOCABLE LETTER OF CREDIT（请开列以下不可撤销信用证）。如果

信用证是保兑或可转让的，应在此加注有关字样。开证方式多为电开(BY TELEX)，也可以是信开、快递或简电开立。

4）L/C NUMBER（信用证号码）。此栏由银行填写。

5）APPLICANT（申请人）。填写申请人的全称及详细地址，有的要求注明联系电话、传真号码等。

6）BENEFICIARY（受益人）。填写受益人的全称及详细地址。

7）ADVISING BANK（通知行）。由开证行填写。

8）AMOUNT（信用证金额）。分别用数字和文字两种形式表示，并且表明币制。如果允许有一定比率的上下浮动，要在信用证中明确表示出来。

9）EXPIRY DATE AND PLACE（到期日期和地点），填写信用证的有效期及到期地点。

10）PARTIAL SHIPMENT（分批装运）、TRANSHIPMENT（转运）。根据合同的实际规定打“×”进行选择。

11）LOADING IN CHARGE、FOR TRANSPORT TO、LATEST DATE OF SHIPMENT（装运地/港、目的地/港的名称，最迟装运日期）。按实际填写，如允许有转运地/港，也应清楚标明。

12）CREDIT AVAILABLE WITH/BY（付款方式）。在所提供的即期、承兑、议付和延期付款四种信用证有效兑付方式中选择与合同要求一致的类型。

13）BENEFICIARY’S DRAFT（汇票要求）。金额应根据合同规定填写：发票金额的一定百分比；发票金额的 100%（全部货款都用信用证支付）；如部分信用证，部分托收时按信用证下的金额比例填写。付款期限可根据实际填写即期或远期，如属后者，必须填写具体的天数。信用证条件下的付款人通常是开证行，也可能是开证行指定的另外一家银行。

14）DOCUMENTS REQUIRED（单据条款）。各银行提供的申请书中已印就的单据条款通常为十几条，从上至下一般为发票、运输单据（提单、空运单、铁路运输单据及运输备忘录等）、保险单、装箱单、质量证书、装运通知和受益人证明等，最后一条是 OTHER DOCUMENTS，IF ANY（其他单据）。如要求提交超过上述所列范围的单据，就可以在此栏填写，如有的合同要求 CERTIFICATE OF NO SOLID WOOD PACKING MATERIAL（无实木包装材料证明）、CERTIFICATE OF FREE SALE（自由销售证明书）、CERTIFICATE OF CONFORMITY（合格证明书）等。申请人填制这部分内容时，应依据合同规定，不能随意增加或减少，选中某单据后对该单据的具体要求（如一式几份、要否签字、正副本的份数、单据中应标明的内容等）也应如实填写，如申请书印制好的要求不完整，应在其后予以补足。

15）COVERING/EVIDENCING SHIPMENT OF（商品描述）。所有内容（品名、规格、包装、单价、唛头）都必须与合同内容相一致，价格条款里附带“AS PER INCOTERMS 2010”、数量条款中规定“MORE OR LESS”或“ABOUT”、使用某种特定包装物等特殊要求必须清楚列明。

16）ADDITIONAL INSTRUCTIONS（附加指示）。该栏通常体现为以下一些条款：

+ALL DOCUMENTS MUST INDICATE CONTRACT NUMBER（所有单据加列合同号码）。

+ALL BANKING CHARGES OUTSIDE THE OPENING BANK ARE FOR BENEFICIARY'S ACCOUNT（开证行以外的所有银行费用由受益人承担）。

+BOTH QUANTITY AND AMOUNT FOR EACH ITEM______ % MORE OR LESS ALLOWED.（每项数量与金额允许______ %增减）。

+THIRD PARTY AS SHIPPER IS NOT ACCEPTABLE.（不接受第三方作为托运人）。

+DOCUMENTS MUST BE PRESNTED WITHIN ××× DAYS AFTER THE DATE OF ISSUANCE OF THE TRANSPORT DOCUMENTS BUT WITHIN THE VALIDITY OF THIS CREDIT.（单据必须在提单日后×××天送达银行并且不超过信用证有效期）。

+SHORT FORM/BLANK BACK/CLAUSED/CHARTER PARTY B/L IS UNACCEPTABLE.（银行不接受略式/不清洁/租船提单）。

+ALL DOCMENTS TO BE FORWARDED IN ONE COVER，UNLESS OTHERWISE STATED ABOVE.（除非有相反规定，所有单据应一次提交）。

+PREPAID FREIGHT DRAWN IN EXCESS OF L/C AMOUNT IS ACCEPTABLE AGAINST PRESENTATION OF ORIGINAL CHARGES VOUCHER ISSUED BY SHIPPING CO./AIR LINE OR ITS AGENT.（银行接受凭船公司/航空公司或其代理人签发的正本运费收据索要超过信用证金额的预付运费）。

+DOCUMENT ISSUED PRIOR TO THE DATE OF ISSUANCE OF CREDIT NOT ACCEPTABLE.（不接受早于开证日出具的单据）。

如需要已印就的上述条款，可在条款前打“×”，对合同涉及但未印就的条款还可以做补充填写。

17）THIS CREDIT IS SUBJECT TO UNIFORM CUSTOMS AND PRACTICE FOR DOCUMENTARY CREDITS (2007 REVISION) INTERNATIONAL CHAMBER OF COMMERCE PUBLICATION No.600. 此信用证遵循国际商会第 600 号出版物《跟单信用证统一惯例》（2007 年版本）。

18）NAME，SIGNATURE OF AUTHORISED PERSON，TEL NO.，FAX，ACCOUNT NO..（授权人名称、签字、电话、传真、账号等内容）。

Reference Application For Documentary Credit:

APPLICATION FOR IRREVOCABLE DOCUMENTARY CREDIT

TO:	Date of Application: 130430
:40A: Please issue an irrevocable documentary letter of credit in the following terms and guarantee back leaf by ☐ airmail ☐ courier ☐ cable ☐ with brief advice by teletransmission ☒full teletransmission	:20 : Credit Number☐☐☐☐☐☐☐☐☐☐☐☐ :31C: Date of Issue YY MM DD

: 50 : Applicant
ZHEJIANG JINHUA Tube Co., Ltd
ROOM 823, WULIN MANSION, WULIN ROAD,
HANGZHOU , ZHEJIANG, P.R.CHINA

: 59 : Beneficiary
PT.DERO INTERNATIONAL
SYAITAM NO.20, KAMPUNG KEDEP DESA TLAJUNG
UDIK KECAMATAN GUNUNG PUTRI KABUPATEN
BOGOR 15862
JAWA BARAT INDONESIA，15862

:43P:Partial Shipments
☐allowed ☒not allowed

:43T: Transshipment
☒allowed ☐not allowed

:44A: Shipment from Jakarta.

44B: Transportation to Ningbo

:44C: Latest Date of Shipment
130605

:57a: Advising Bank

:31D: Date of Expiry on 130620
Place of Expiry in INDONESIA______

:32B: Currency Code, Amount
USD 600,000.00 SAY U.S DOLLARS SIX HANDRED THOUSAND ONLY.

:39A: Percentage Credit Amount Tolerance
10%

:41a: Credit available with ☐adv. bank ☒any bank in _INDONESIA____
by ☐ sight payment ☐ acceptance ☒negotiation ☐ mixed payment ☐ deferred payment at____________days

:42C: against presentation of the documents and beneficiary's draft(s)
at***_______sight

:42a: drawn on us for 100 % of invoice value

:46a: Documents Required (marked with X)
☒Signed commercial Invoice in __3__ copies indicating this credit number and contract number.
☒ Full set of clean " On Board" Ocean (☒ Bills of Lading ☐ Cargo Receipt) made out to (☐ you ☒ order) and blank endorsed, marked" Freight (☐prepaid ☐paid ☒collect)" , and notifying (☒the applicant ☐_______________)
☐ (☐Airway Bills ☐Railway Bills) showing " Freight (☐prepaid ☐paid ☐collect)" and consigned to
☐ Full set of Insurance Policy / Certificate for 110 % of the invoice value, showing claims payable in China, in the currency of the draft, and blank endorsed, covering (☐ ocean marine transportation ☐ air transportation ☐overland transportation) All Risks and War Risks.
☒Packing List / Weight Memo in __3__ copies issued by __the beneficiary__ indicating quantity / gross and net weights of each package and packing conditions as called by this credit.
☒ Certificate of Quantity / Weight in 1 copies issued by the surveyor indicating the actual surveyed quantity / weight of shipped goods as well as the packing conditions.
☐ Certificate of Quality in ____________ copies issued by ____________
☐ Certificate of Origin in ____________ copies issued by ____________
☒Beneficiary's certified copy of Fax / telex dispatched to the applicant within __48__ hours
Before shipment advising (☒name of vessel /☐flight number / ☐wagon number), date of shipment, name, quantity, weight and value of goods.
☒ Beneficiary's Certificate certifying that extra copies of documents dispatched to the applicant directly according to the contract terms
☐

:45a: Description of Goods
Plastic Granule OB Jakarta
200tons PP ,
200tons LLDPE,
200tons HDPE

Packing
In Plastic Bag , 40 ft Container , Export Standard
Shipping Mark
N/M
Price Term ☒FOB ☐CFR ☐CIF ☐

:49: Confirmation Instruction ☒confirm ☐without confirm ☐may add confirm	
:71B: All banking charges outside the opening bank are for beneficiary's account.	
:48: Documents must be presented within 15 days after the date of issuance of the transport documents but within the validity of this credit.	
:47a: Additional Conditions ☒ Third party as shipper and short form / blank back B/L are not acceptable. ☒ Documents must be forwarded in ☒ one ☐ two lot(s), unless stated. ☐	Applicant's Signature and Seal Contact with: Tel:

Task 5 Requesting Documents

Writing Background

印度尼西亚 PT.DERO International 公司按照合同规定及时发出了第一批 60 吨塑料粒子。

Writing task

浙江嘉华管业有限公司为了早日收到塑料粒子，加工管材，希望 PT.DERO International 公司尽快把信用证项下所需单据递交银行。请代表嘉华公司撰写该邮件。

Reference E-mail

Dear Huma,

Very happy to know you have shipped the goods. Thank you very much.

We hope you can present the relevant documents under the L/C as soon as possible, as we rush processing.

Best Regards,

Lily

Task 6 Signing S/C

Writing Background

浙江嘉华管业有限公司已经完成了第一批塑料粒子的进口，为了加工的成品管材能够及时出口，他们积极与海外老顾客联系，最终俄罗斯客商给他们发来了订单（当然，在进料加工的贸易方式下，中方公司应该在向海关申请办理进料加工手册时，就提交进口原料和出口成品的双向合同。然而为了业务的连贯性，编者把签订出口合同作为该情境的第六个任务）。

Writing task

请根据下列俄罗斯客户的订单，起草一份管材出口合同。

Order No	ST13015	Date	June 5, 2013
Commodity	PAP (Pex-AL-Pex) pipe		
Specification	1. working pressure: 1.25Mpa[7] 2. outer diameter(mm): 25; Thickness: 2.3mm; Length: 100-300m 3. Life Span: more than 50 years		
Packing	in coils packed with water proof paper		
Price Term	CIF ST.Petersburg Amount: USD180 000.00		
Unit Price	USD1.8/Meter		
Quantity	100 000Meters		
Shipment	30 days after receipt of L/C allowing transhipments and partial shipment.		
Payment	by 100% confirmed irrevocable letter of credit in the seller's favor available by draft at sight.		
Insurance	Covered by the seller.		

Reference Sales Contract:

SALES CONTRACT

编号 S/C No.：JH1321
日期 Date: June 10, 2013
签约地点 Signed At : Shanghai, China

卖方 Sellers：ZHEJIANG JINHUA Tube Co., Ltd.
ROOM 823, WULIN MANSION
WULIN ROAD, HANGZHOU
ZHEJIANG, P.R.CHINA

买方 Buyers：SNOW TRADING COMPANY
A, KORP.3, 22, STAKHANOVSKAYA UL., G.
KOLPINO RU-186653 STAINT PETERSBURG
RUSSIAN FEDERATION

兹买卖双方同意成交下列商品，双方订立条款如下：

The contract is made by and agreed between the buyer and the seller in accodance with the terms and conditions stupilated below:

1. 品名及规格 Name of Commodity and Specification	2. 数量 Quantity	3. 单价及价格条款 Unit Price	4. 总金额 Total Amount USD
PAP (Pex-AL-Pex) pipe	100 000Meters	CIF ST.Petersburg USD1.8/ meter	180 000.00

5. 数量及总值均可有 10%的增减，由卖方决定。

With 10% more or less both in amount and quantity allowed at the Seller's option.

6. 包装 Packing：用防水纸成圈包装。In coils packed with water proof paper.

7. 装运期限：☑ 收到信用证后一个月内发货，允许转运和分批装运。

Time of Shipment: ☑ One month after receipt of your L/C allowing transshipment and partial shipment.

8. 装运口岸：上海。

Port of Loading: Shanghai.

9. 目的港：圣彼得堡。

Port of Destination: ST.Petersburg

10. 付款条件：☑ 100%保兑的不可撤销的即期信用证付款，以卖方为受益人。

Terms of Payment: ☑ By 100% confirmed irrevocable letter of credit in our favor available by draft at sight.

11. 保险：☑按中国保险条款，投保一切险及战争险。

Insurance: ☑ Covering All Risks and War Risk as per the China Insurance Clauses.

12. 装船标记 Shipping Marks: N/M.

13. 备注（REMARKS）

卖方	买方
THE SELLERS	THE BUYERS
ZHEJIANG JINHUA Tube Co., Ltd.	SNOW TRADING COMPANY

Task 7 Sending shipping advice

Writing Background

合同签订后不久，浙江嘉华管业有限公司就收到了俄罗斯 Snow Trading Company 通过银行开来的相关信用证。经审核，信用证条款没有问题，所以嘉华公司在信用证规定的时间之内完成了发货。

Writing task

请撰写一份装船通知，发给俄罗斯 Snow Trading Company，以便他们及时安排接货。

Reference E-mail

Jane,

Happy to tell you that your goods have been shipped on July 20, 2013. The following is the shiping information:

Invoice No.:2013Jh21
Quantity: 100 000 Meters
B/L No. : FEGU24536789
Port of Shipment : SHANGHAI
Port of Destination: ST. PETERSBURG
Ocean Vessel: BLUE V.063B
Container/Seal Number: HGTD405732/JFT953
KFTY956743/HGD875
SETD876453/UTD364

Best Regards,
Lily

Task 8 Transaction Review

Writing Background

浙江嘉华管业有限公司终于顺利完成了第一笔进料加工业务，从印度尼西亚进口塑料粒子，加工成管材出口俄罗斯。

Writing task

请代表浙江嘉华管业有限公司撰写两封邮件，分别发给印度尼西亚的出口商和俄罗斯的进口商，回顾愉快的交易过程，希望再次合作。

Reference E-mails

For PT.DERO International:

Dear Huma，

Glad to tell you that we are satisfactory to your plastic granule and hope to cooperate with you next time.

Best Regards,
Lily

For Snow Trading Company:

Jane,

How are you ?

I would like to check with you about the distribution of PAP pipe. If you have purchsing plan for pipe or fittings, please contact me without delay. Thank you !

Looking forward to cooperation next time !

Best Regards,

Lily

Notes

1. PP：聚丙烯，英文 Polypropylene 的缩写，是由丙烯聚合而制得的一种热塑性树脂。PP 管材主要用作农用输水管。采用进口 PP-R 料生产的输送冷、热水用的管材目前普遍得到市场认可。据悉，目前国产 PP-R 料与进口料比较还有一定差距，质量有待改进和提高。

2. LLDPE：线型低密度聚乙烯，Linear Low-Density Polyethy -lene 的英文缩写。聚乙烯（PE）是五大合成树脂之一，是我国合成树脂中产能最大、进口量最多的品种。聚乙烯主要分为线型低密度聚乙烯（LLDPE）、低密度聚乙烯（LDPE）、高密度聚乙烯（HDPE）三大类。LLDPE 已进入聚乙烯的大多数传统市场，包括薄膜、模塑、管材和电线电缆。LLDPE 薄膜具有下列性能：热封性能、熔融性能、热性能和物理力学性能。

3. HDPE：高密度聚乙烯，High-Density Polyethy-lene 的英文缩写。HDPE 是一种结晶度高、非极性的热塑性树脂。原态 HDPE 的外表呈乳白色，在微薄截面呈一定程度的半透明状。

4. 40 ft Container：40 英尺普通货柜，是 40 feet container 的缩写。它的内容积为 11.8 米×2.13 米×2.18 米，配货毛重一般为 22 吨，体积为 54 立方米。

5. PO：订购单，是 Purchase Order 的缩写。

6. DHL：DHL（敦豪航空货运公司）是一家创立自美国，目前为德国与美国合资的速递货运公司，是目前世界上最大的航空速递货运公司之一。1969 年，DHL 开设了他们的第一条从旧金山到檀香山的速递运输航线，快递公司的名称“DHL”由三位创始人姓氏的首字母组成（Dalsey, Hillblom and Lynn）。敦豪航空货运公司于中国大陆因合作伙伴关系称为中外运敦豪；而在中国台湾部分，其早年进入中国台湾时曾使用洋基通运的译名，但为了企业识别的统一，目前已舍弃中文名称不用，直接称呼为 DHL；在中国香港，公司的正式注册名称为敦豪国际，但日常仍然使用 DHL。

7. Mpa：压强单位兆帕斯卡。1 标准大气压=0.1MPa=760mmHG 水银柱；1 大气压=1.03323kg/cm^2 的压力；1MPA=10 大气压力=10.3323kg/cm^2；即相当于 10.332 公斤/平方厘米的压力。

Important Words and Phrases

1. PAP (Pex-AL-Pex) pipe　　铝塑复管材
2. PP-R Pipe　　PP-R 管材

3. Compress Fittings 铝塑复管件
4. PVC pipe clamp PVC 管卡
5. Press Fittings 压合管件
6. Valves 阀门
7. Purifie 净水器
8. Tape 生料带
9. Water Meter 水表
10. Processing with Imported Materials 进料加工
11. the Yangtze River Delta Economic Circle 长三角经济圈
12. competitive mechanism 竞争机制
13. marching into overseas markets 进军海外市场
14. plastic granule 塑料粒子
15. Attachment 用电子邮件发送的附件
16. working pressure 工作压力
17. outer diameter 外径
18. Life Span 寿命
19. in coils packed with water proof paper 用防水纸成圈包装
20. 40' HQ 40 尺高柜
21. step up production 增加产量
22. heavy enquiries 大量询盘
23. distribution channels 销售渠道
24. trade circles 贸易界
25. compensation trade 补偿贸易
26. processing trade 来料加工贸易
27. assembling trade 来料装配贸易
28. leasing trade 租赁贸易
29. trade agreement 贸易协议
30. fluctuate in line with market conditions 随行就市

Useful Expressions

1. In case of short shipment, you can lodge a claim with the shipowner or with the insurance company.
2. Please look into the case at once.
3. If you have any inquiries, please feel free to contact us by any means of communication available.
4. You can visit our website to get more online information.
5. Please find the payment receipt in attachment.
6. To be candid with you, we have no magin to cut the price down again.

7. We have to recheck the price and see if we can accept your counter-offer.

8. Do you have promotion plan before Christmas?

9. It is our peak season before our CNY(Chinese New year) holiday.

10. In other words, you could help us to open up the European market.

11. Sorry to inform you that I will no longer handle the processing trade due to the internal transfer.

12. Due to the quality problem, we'll stop doing business with your company.

13. Please go and visit our website for new products.

14. Please call my mobile for any top urgent issues.

15. We'll arrange the production as soon as we receive your approval e-mail.

16. Good price! But we cannot accept your package. We would order 10 000pcs if you pack the goods according to our requirement.

17. As this is the first order between us, it is impossible for us to place a large quantity.

18. We'd like to know what you can supply as well as your sales conditions.

19. He inquired about the style, size, color and price of the colthing.

20. We always have faith in the quality of your products.

Exercises

1. 下面是一个潜在客户的询盘，请对询盘进行回复。

Dear Sirs,

We are interested in your hardwares and would like to have details of your prices and terms. Looking forward to hearing from you.

Yours Faithfully,

Tom

2. 请根据下列销售合同填写开证申请书。

SALES CONTRACT

编号 S/C No.：JH1321

日期 Date: June 10, 2013

签约地点 Signed At : Shanghai, China

卖方 Sellers：ZHEJIANG LANTIAN IMPORT AND EXPORT CO., LTD.
108 JIEFANG STREET, HANGZHOU, CHINA

买方 Buyers：NELTEXCO LIMITED
5 KING ROAD, DUBAI, U.A.E.

兹买卖双方同意成交下列商品，双方订立条款如下：

The contract is made by and agreed between the buyer and the seller in accodance with the terms and conditions stupilated below:

1）品名及规格 Name of Commodity and Specification	2）数量 Quantity	3）单价及价格条款 Unit Price	4）总金额 Total Amount USD
Jacket	3000pcs	CIF Dubai USD20/ pc	60 000.00

5. 数量及总值均可有 5%的增减，由卖方决定。

With 5% more or less both in amount and quantity allowed at the Seller's option.

6. 包装 Packing：每单位出口标准箱装 20 件。20 pcs are packed in one export standard carton.

7. 装运期限：☑ 收到信用证后一个月内发货，不允许转运和分批装运。

Time of Shipment: ☑ One month after receipt of your L/C not allowing transshipment and partial shipment.

8. 装运口岸：上海。

Port of Loading: Shanghai.

9. 目的港：迪拜。

Port of Destination: Dubai

10. 付款条件：☑ 100%保兑的不可撤销的即期信用证付款，以卖方为受益人。

Terms of Payment: ☑ By 100% confirmed irrevocable letter of credit in our favor available by draft at sight.

11. 保险：☑按中国保险条款，投保一切险及战争险。

Insurance: ☑ Covering All Risks and War Risk as per the China Insurance Clauses.

12. 装船标记 Shipping Marks: N/M.

13. 备注（REMARKS）

卖方	买方
THE SELLERS	THE BUYERS
ZHEJIANG LANTIAN IMPORT AND EXPORT CO., LTD.	NELTEXCO LIMITED

3. 请撰写一份离职通知（Resignation Announcement）给业务伙伴，内容包括：

1）由于某些原因需要离开现在的公司；

2）感谢对方多年来对你工作的支持；

3）希望继续保持联系。

Study Situation 3

3.1 General Agency

Business Background:

浙江万德福洁具有限公司与比利时 Star International Trading Est 公司经过多次合作后，应比利时 Star International Trading Est 公司的请求，授权其为洁具产品在比利时的一般代理。

Business Requirements:

1. 熟悉公司情况和卫生洁具行业产品信息，尤其是淋浴房设施信息。
2. 学习考察合作商资质，合理选择代理商。
3. 会写业务善后函，能够运用函电推陈出新，挖掘更多交易机会，维护客户关系。
4. 能够运用函电与老客户进行一般代理磋商。
5. 熟悉一般代理协议条款，会起草一般代理协议。

Teaching Objective:

培养学生运用函电向老客户推介洁具新产品、进行一般代理磋商及起草一般代理协议的能力。

Company Profile

Zhejiang Wonderful Sanitary Wares Co., Ltd. was established in 1985, located at the Lingang Industrial Park, Hangzhou City, Zhejiang Province. It is only 10 minutes' ride from Xiaoshan International Airport. The company covers an area of 30 000 square meters, including five modern standard workshops and one comprehensive office building. It is a professional manufacturer and exporter of shower cabins, shower enclosures, steam showers, massage bathtubs and shower panels, etc.. The company has successfully gained ISO 9001:2001 International Quality System Certificate and CE Certificate.

We have been in this line for over 30 years. In our factory, fully automatic production lines are adopted for big orders' mass production, which we believe can make the production cost as low as possible and therefore our prices will be more competitive.

For instance, producing shower enclosures 2 000pcs per model in one order will be much more economical than producing 200pcs per model once our automatic production line is started.

Therefore, if you order 2 000pcs shower panels per model in one order, the unit price will be lower than that to other customers who buy 200pcs per model.

We welcome trial orders and hope that buyers will place orders as large as possible for each model so that your purchasing cost will be lowered.

If you have any inquiries, please feel free to contact us by any means of communication available. Also you can visit our website to get more online information. Once you choose us, you will enjoy our good quality products with the lowest price and the best service. We will try to make your business more profitable and help expand market faster.

Holding the motto of quality and credit priority, we sincerely welcome your visit and cooperation for a wonderful future!

Task1 Transaction Review

Writing Background

浙江万德福洁具有限公司与比利时Star International Trading Est公司最近又成功完成了一笔交易，双方有意开展进一步合作。

Writing Task

请以浙江万德福洁具有限公司总经理 Helen Zhang 的名义给比利时 Star International Trading Est 公司去函，对最近一笔业务进行回顾，并借机推介公司新产品。比利时 Star International Trading Est 公司的联络人：

John Jordan
General Manager
STAR INTERNATIONAL TRADING EST
AV. R.VANDER BRUGGEN 43
BRUSSELS, BELGIUM

Reference E-mail

Dear Mr. Jordan,

We are pleased to know that the issuing bank has honored our draft against L/C No. 2013JHPJLM.

You can be sure that the goods shipped will meet your needs just well. We believe the conclusion of this transaction will help to further our mutual understanding and pave the way for more business in the future.

Enclosed is our latest catalogue, in which you may find quite a few new items. If you have any further requirement, please inform us A.S.A.P.

We would like to assure you of our prompt and careful attention in handling your future orders.

Yours Truly,
Zhejiang Wonderful Sanitary Wares Co., Ltd.
Helen Zhang
General Manager

Task 2 Negotiation on General Agency

Writing Background

比利时 Star International Trading Est 公司总经理给浙江万德福洁具有限公司总经理 Helen Zhang 回函，表达了想担任万德福洁具有限公司在比利时销售其淋浴房产品的一般代理的愿望。信函正文如下：

Dear Helen,

Thank you for your letter dated Nov. 21, 2013. We have carefully read the enclosed catalogue, and we are sure there will be more business opportunities between our two companies.

As you know, we have a well-developed sales organization in Belgium and are represented by a large staff in various parts of the country. From their reports, it seems clear that there is a good demand for your shower rooms and as we believe you are not directly represented in Belgium, we are writing to offer our service as your general agent.

There are good prospects of a very profitable market for your manufactures. Provided terms could be arranged, we think our 15 years' experience in this line should enable us to work up a very satisfactory business with you.

In view of our successful transactions for so many times which we are fortunate enough to possess, we think you will agree that a 6 percent commission on net sales is quite reasonable. We are also prepared to guarantee payment of all accounts.

We hope to hear favourably from you and feel sure that we could come to an agreement as to terms.

Best Regards,
John

Writing Task

请以浙江万德福洁具有限公司总经理 Helen Zhang 的名义进行回复，表示对比利时方面的提议甚感兴趣，并希望对方派员前来中国商讨代理事宜。

Writing Guide

Agents play an important role in foreign trade. When appointing an agent, we (the principal) must be cautious about the qualification, experience and personal quality of the agent in order to avoid subsequent trouble. It is a good policy to make searching enquiries through reliable sources such as our commercial counselor's office and our banks for the needful information before entering into an agreement.

E-mails concerning agency matters are not necessarily long, but the purpose of the letter must be clear. Of course, courtesy is required in our correspondence. The conclusion of an agreement is the product of compromise. It needs time and patience. To enter into an agreement based on one's own wishful thinking is not advisable or even impossible. An old saying goes, "if a small thing is not well treated, big trouble will arise."

The language used in such correspondence can be straight. We can feel free to decline a request for sole agency if the terms and conditions of both parties are not in line, or the firm which applies to be our agent fails to meet our expected requirements.

Reference E-mail

Dear John,

Thanks for your prompt reply. As for your proposal to be our general agent in Belgium for shower rooms, we are quite interested in that actually.

As there should be a lot more details to be discussed, we sincerely hope that you or someone authorized will come to China by the end of this year. We believe that your visit will make our business more constructive.

We are looking forward to hearing from you soon.

Thanks and Best Regards,
Helen

Task 3 Drafting a General Agency Agreement

Writing Background

次月初，比利时 Star International Trading Est 公司总经理 John Jordan 先生飞往中国，与浙江万德福洁具有限公司就淋浴房产品一般代理协议条款的问题进行了认真磋商。

Writing task

请为浙江万德福洁具有限公司草拟一份一般代理协议。

Writing Guide

Drafting a formal agreement is a matter that calls for great care. All the details to be included must be unanimously agreed by both parties.

A formal agreement may include all, or some, of the following terms:

① Preamble;

② The nature of the agreement;

③ The name of commodity and specifications;

④ The territory to be covered;

⑤ The method of purchase & sale (special provisions);

⑥ Mode of payment;

⑦ Details of commission and expenses to be allowed;

⑧ The duties of agent and principal;

⑨ Arbitration and court jurisdiction in the event of disputes;

⑩ The language used;

⑪ The governing law;

⑫ Validity of the agreement;

⑬ Witness clause: In witness thereof, this agreement is signed on … by both parties in two original copies; each party holds one copy.

Reference Agreement

GENERAL AGENCY AGREEMENT

This agreement is entered into between the parties concerned on the basis of equality and mutual benefit to develop business on terms and conditions mutually agreed upon as follows:

1. The Parties Concerned

Supplier: ZHEJIANG WONDERFUL SANITARY WARES CO., LTD.
ROOM 2501, JIAFA MANSTION, YANAN ROAD
HANGZHOU, P.R.CHINA
Postal Code: 320005
Tel: 086-571-82333088
Fax: 086-571-82333089
(Hereinafter called Party A)

Agent: STAR INTERNATIONAL TRADING EST
AV. R.VANDER BRUGGEN 43, BRUSSELS, BELGIUM
(Hereinafter called Party B)

Party A hereby appoints Party B to act as its General Agent to sell the commodity mentioned bellow.

2. Commodity and Quantity

Wonderful Brand Shower rooms of all specifications.

It is mutually agreed that Party B shall undertake the sales of the aforesaid commodity for not less than 5 000 sets in the duration of the agreement.

3. Territory

BELGIUM.

4. Validity of Agreement

This agreement when duly signed by the parties concerned shall remain in force for 12 calendar months to be effective January 1st, 2014 to December 31st, 2014, and it will be extended for another 12 months upon its expiration unless notice is given to the contrary.

5. Confirmation of Orders

Party B shall submit offers to other parties completely in accordance with the specifications and trade terms given by Party A and is not allowed to make any alteration without Party A's permission. The commission on each transaction is to be fixed through mutual consultation and paid to Party B after full payment of the transaction has been received by Party A. Every transaction concluded is binding only after it is confirmed by Party A in writing.

6. Reports on Market Conditions

Party B shall have the obligation to forward once every three months to Party A detailed reports on current market conditions and of consumer's comments, and if there is any special change in the market. Party B shall also report timely to Party A its full particulars in writing.

7. Payment

Payment is to be made by confirmed, irrevocable letter of credit, without recourse, available by draft at sight upon presentation of shipping documents to the negotiation bank in China. The letter of credit for each order, whether opened by the agent or by the customer, shall reach Party A 30 days before the date of shipment.

8. Other Terms and Conditions

1) During the validity of this agreement, Party A shall not make offers of the said goods to any party in the above-mentioned territory other than Party B, and Party B shall guarantee not to undertake the agency of, or to handle the sale of, the same kind of goods for any other countries.

2) Party B must be responsible for placing orders and arranging L/C to be opened in favour of Party A for at least 2 500 sets for the first six months and 2 500 sets for the second six months of the duration of this agreement. Should Party B fail to pass on orders to Party A for a minimum quantity of 2 500 sets for the first six month, Party A shall have the right to sell the same goods to any other buyers.

3) It is understood that this general agency agreement does not involve the transactions concluded in the following ways:

① Transactions concluded by Party A in the name of its government on one side with the government of Party B on the other.

② Transactions concluded between Party A and any other buyers in Belgium for goods to be re-exported to other countries.

4) When a transaction is confirmed by Party A, Party B is held responsible for its fulfillment.

5) Party A has the right to revise or change the selling prices in accordance with the prevailing market conditions and shall notify Party B of the change in time.

6) During the validity of this agreement, if either of the two parties is found to have infringed the stipulations of the agreement, the other party has the right to terminate this agreement by giving notice in writing to the infringing party.

Party A (Supplier)	Party B (Agent)
ZHEJIANG WONDERFUL SANITARY WARES CO., LTD.	STAR INTERNATIONAL TRADING EST

Important Words and Phrases

1. agent	代理人
2. in treaty with	与某人接洽
3. hinge on (upon)	依靠
4. modify	更改
5. withdraw	撤销
6. premature	未成熟的；为时过早的
7. misinterpret	误解
8. turnover	营业额
9. warrant	保证
10. expiration	满期
11. revise	修改
12. prevail	盛行，占优势
13. infringe	违反
14. designate	指定
15. without recourse	不可追索的
16. preamble	前文，序言
17. special provisions	特殊条款
18. principal	委托人
19. jurisdiction	司法权，审判权，管辖权
20. governing law	适用法律

Useful Expressions

1. We are glad to know that the issuing bank has honored our draft against L/C No. AJYK521.

2. We hope this deal will be the basis of the further development of our business relationship.

3. We can ensure that you will find the goods shipped to your entire satisfaction. We are looking forward to your repeat orders.

4. We trust that through our joint efforts, we will have a more profitable future.

5. We would like to take this opportunity to recommend to you our new products.

6. We are very concerned to receive the Notification of Dishonor from the issuing bank.

7. We feel deeply sorry for the mistake in our negotiation documents, which is made as a result of our clerk's carelessness.

8. We really hope this incident will not affect negatively our friendly cooperation.

9. We can guarantee that the quantity of the goods is exactly in line with the stipulations of the relevant contract.

10. Since our goods have been shipped on time, would you be kind enough to make the payment through your bank?

11. With your excellent connections, we believe it will be possible to promote the sale of our products in your territory, and we hope your acting as our agent will be to our mutual benefit.

12. Referring to the question of agency, we are not yet prepared to consider this matter. We shall, however, revert to it when (as soon as) business develops (has developed) to our mutual satisfaction.

13. Regarding your proposal to represent us in South Africa for the sale of Yongkang Hardware, we have decided to appoint you as our agent.

14. We appreciate your proposal to act as our general agent for…, but we have already appointed… as our agent in your city.

15. We have noted your request to act as our agent in your district, but before going further into the matter, we should like to know your plan for promoting sales and the annual turnover you may realize in your market.

16. We feel it would be better to consider the matter of agency after you have done more business with us.

17. The time is not yet mature for the discussion of agency.

18. In consideration of your extensive experience in the field, we are glad to appoint you as our general agent.

19. Thank you for your proposal of acting as our general agent.

20. If we come to terms, we'll appoint you as our general agent.

Exercises

1. 请根据下述资料拟写一封英文函电。

You are not satisfied with the sales volume your agent in Canada brought to you last year. Send an E-mail to the agent for a full report on the matter and what measures the agent intends to take to improve sales. Point out tactfully that business cannot be continued unless a higher level of sales is reached.

2. 将下列句子译成英文。

1）对你方提议担任我方酒店用品一般代理一事，深表感谢。鉴于彼此尚不熟悉，我方认为待达成一些实际交易之后再来考虑此事较为妥当。

2）待贵司销售业绩有明显增长后，我方将考虑委托贵司担任一般代理。

3）可否通告贵司的推销计划以及你处市场的每年销售量，这将对我们有很大帮助。

4）经考虑你方的提议以及调查了你方的业务情况以后，兹决定以下列条款为准，委托你方在提议的地区内作为我方的一般代理。

5）一旦达成协议，你方必须保证每月订购一定数量，如此我方才能确保经常供货。

3. 自选途径，查阅一份一般代理协议，并将之翻译成中文。

3.2 Sole Agency

Business Background

浙江永康爱家燃气灶具制造有限公司主要生产各种型号和规格的炉头和燃气灶具，产品远销美国、日本、加拿大、法国、巴西、沙特阿拉伯、约旦、韩国、泰国、马来西亚等国家，深受客户青睐。其中，加拿大三合厨具贸易有限公司与永康爱家燃气灶具制造有限公司已有多次成功的贸易往来，决定再次与后者进行接洽，商讨在加拿大独家代理其生产的燃气灶具产品的可能性。

Business Requirements

1. 熟悉公司情况和厨具行业产品信息，尤其是燃气灶具。
2. 进一步学习和应用代理商选择策略。
3. 掌握业务善后函的写作流程。
4. 能够运用函电与老客户进行独家代理磋商。
5. 熟悉独家代理协议条款，能起草独家代理协议。

Teaching Objective

培养学生运用函电向老客户推介厨具新产品、进行独家代理磋商及起草独家代理协议的能力。

Company Profile

Zhejiang Yongkang Aijia Gas Cooker Manufacturing Co., Ltd. is one of the biggest enterprises in the line of making and selling gas cookers and other kitchen utensils in China. Since its foundation in 1998, it has always attached much importance to quality control, technological innovation and staff management, which has made it take up the leading position in the development and technique of European-style products and even win the approval and respect of its competitors. It has acquired the certification of ISO 9001: 2000, CCC, European CE, American UL and Singapore PSB certification.

Its main products furnace end and gas cooker have been granted the honor of "National Famous Brand" by the authorities. Since its establishment, its products have always found ready markets both home and abroad and have got sound reputation in this field. At present, it is sharing a good market in America, Japan, Canada, France, Brazil, Saudi Arabia, Jordan, South Korea, Thailand, Malaysia, etc..

Under the new marketing circumstances, the enterprise will constantly implement technological innovation and provide quality products and services for its clients.

Task 1 Transaction Review

Writing Background

浙江永康爱家燃气灶具制造有限公司与加拿大三合厨具贸易有限公司已有过多次愉快的合作经历。最近双方又成功达成一笔交易。浙江永康爱家燃气灶具制造有限公司外贸部业务员胡萍（Jessica）刚收到加拿大三合厨具贸易有限公司的货款。

Writing Task

请你以浙江永康爱家燃气灶具制造有限公司外贸部业务员胡萍（Jessica）的名义，给加拿大三合厨具贸易有限公司业务代表 Royan 发一封电子邮件，说明已成功收到货款，并向其推介新产品。

Reference E-mail

Dear Royan,

We are glad to know that the issuing bank has honored our draft of USD93 569.00 against L/C No. YK-LC-20130426 under Contract No. AJ-20130410. You can be sure that the goods shipped will meet your needs just as the former transactions between us.

As you are a leading company in Canada with many years' experience in kitchen utensils business, we are expecting more communications on business with you. And we believe the successful transactions will further help to improve our relationship in the future.

Perhaps you are not aware of our new series of flush bonding(嵌入式)products with many specifications, so we enclosed an illustrated catalogue for your consideration. If your order exceed USD100 000，we will give you a favorable discount.

Please let us know if any new item interests you. We appreciate any comments on our products and we are looking forward to your more specific enquiries.

Regards,
Jessica

加拿大三合厨具贸易有限公司业务代表 Royan 收到邮件后给胡萍作了如下回复。

Hi Jessica,

Thank you for your E-mail dated on June 11, 2013. The pleasure is also ours. We are now expecting the goods sailing in the Pacific Ocean. And we believe that they will always be to our entire satisfaction.

We have closely studied your new catalogue, and are quite interested in some models of flush bonding series. We are considering new enquires to you after putting the former shipment into the ready market.

We are very happy to tell you that our MD[2] Mr. Sugat would like to negotiate the possibility of acting as the sole agent of your gas cooker series in Canada. He will e-mail your Export Manager soon.

Regards,
Royan

Task 2 Negotiation on Sole Agency

Writing Background

加拿大三合厨具贸易有限公司市场总监 Sugat 先生给浙江永康爱家燃气灶具制造有限公司外贸部经理应丽君女士（Suzanna）发了一封电子邮件，表达了要求担任“爱家”牌燃气灶具加拿大独家代理的愿望。

Dear Suzanna,

How have you been? Hope everything is OK with you just as the satisfactory cooperation between our two companies.

I think that it’s about time for us to further develop the kitchen utensils business in Canada. Here we’d like to know if there is any possibility of us being the sole agent in Canada for your gas cookers. And I bet that you know our qualifications for that quite well.

In two weeks’ time I will fly to Shanghai for a short stay. And surely I will be very pleased to visit your company. I am waiting with interest for your decision.

Best Wishes,

Sugat

Writing Task

请以浙江永康爱家燃气灶具制造有限公司外贸部经理应丽君女士（Suzanna）的名义回复电子邮件给 Sugat 先生，说明浙江永康爱家燃气灶具制造有限公司对加拿大三合厨具贸易有限公司的提议甚感兴趣，欢迎其亲自前来洽谈有关独家代理协议的各项事项。

Dear Mr. Sugat,

We duly received your E-mail of June 17th, 2013 and after careful consideration of the contents, we are favourably impressed with your proposal to act as our sole agent.

We have already been in treaty with several companies, but at present have come to no decision in the issue. However, if terms could be arranged, we think you would be just the people we should like to represent us. We believe you have good connections throughout the trade, and it seems to us a favourable opportunity to further develop the business in Canada.

Of course, the whole matter hinges upon the question of the amount of commission you would require on orders obtained and executed. Since you will visit Shanghai in a fortnight's time, we think we should prefer to discuss the various points with you personally, instead of stating general conditions and terms which would probably have to be modified or withdrawn after an interview.

We shall, therefore, await your call.

Best Regards,

Suzanna

Task 3 Drafting a Sole Agency Agreement

Writing Background

半个月后，Sugat 先生如期来到中国，并代表加拿大三合厨具贸易有限公司与浙江永康爱家燃气灶具制造有限公司高层接洽。双方经过谈判，成功签订了独家代理协议。

Writing task

请为浙江永康爱家燃气灶具制造有限公司草拟一份独家代理协议。

SOLE AGENCY AGREEMENT

This agreement is made and entered into by and between the parties concerned on July 8, 2013 in Yongkang Zhejiang, China on the basis of equality and mutual benefit to develop business on terms and conditions mutually agreed upon as follows:

1. The Parties Concerned

Supplier: Zhejiang Yongkang Aijia Gas Cooker Manufacturing Co., Ltd.
1188 Industry Road
Yongkang City, Zhejiang Province, P.R.China
Postal Code: 321000
Tel: 086-579-87063069
Fax: 086-579-87065883
(Hereinafter called Party A)

Agent: Trio Kitchen Utensils Trading Incorporation
Montreal, Quebec, Canada
H2N 2G1
Tel: 001-514-3994455
Fax: 001-514-3994456
(Hereinafter called Party B)

2. Appointment

Party A hereby appoints Party B as its Exclusive/Sole Agent to solicit orders for the commodity stipulated in Article 3 from customers in the territory stipulated in Article 4, and Party B accepts and assumes such an appointment.

3. Commodity

"Aijia Brand" Gas Cookers of all specifications.

4. Territory

In Canada only.

5. Minimum Turnover

Party B shall undertake to solicit orders for the above commodity from customers in the above territory during the effective period of this agreement for not less than USD200 000.00.

6. Price and Payment

The price for each individual transaction shall be fixed through negotiations between Party B and the buyer, and subject to Party A's final confirmation.

Payment shall be made by confirmed, irrevocable L/C opened by the buyer in favor of Party A, which shall reach Party A 15 days before the date of shipment.

7. Exclusive Right

In consideration of the exclusive rights granted herein, Party A shall not, directly or indirectly, sell or export the commodity stipulated in Article 4 to customers in Canada through channels other than Party B; Party B shall not sell, distribute or promote the sales of any products competitive with or similar to the above commodity in Canada and shall not solicit or accept orders for the purpose of selling them outside Canada. Party A shall refer to Party B any enquiries or orders for the commodity in question received by Party A from other firms in

Canada during the validity of this agreement.

8. Market Report

In order to keep Party A well informed of the prevailing market conditions, Party B should undertake to supply Party A, at least once a quarter or at any time when necessary, with market reports concerning changes of the local regulations in connection with the import and sales of the commodity covered by this agreement, local market tendency and the buyer's comments on quality, packing, price, etc. of the goods supplied by Party A under this agreement. Party B shall also supply party A with quotations and advertising materials on similar products of other suppliers.

9. Advertising and Expenses

Party A shall bear all expenses for advertising and publicity in connection with the commodity in question in Canada within the validity of this agreement, and shall submit to Party A all audio and video materials intended for advertising for prior approval.

10. Commission

Party A shall pay Party B a commission of 5% on the net invoiced selling price on all orders directly obtained by Party B and accepted by party A. No commission shall be paid until Party A receives the full payment for each order.

11. Transactions between Governmental Bodies

Transactions concluded between governmental bodies of Party A and Party B shall not be restricted by the terms and conditions of this agreement, nor shall the amount of such transactions be counted as part of the turnover stipulated in Article 5.

12. Industrial Property Rights

Party B may use the trade-marks owned by Party A for the sale of the Aijia Brand Gas Cookers covered herein within the validity of this agreement, and shall acknowledge that all patents, trademarks, copy rights or any other industrial property rights used or embodied in the Aijia Brand Gas Cookers shall remain to be the sole properties of Party A. Should any infringement be found, Party B shall promptly notify and assist Party A to take steps to protect the latter's rights.

13. Validity of Agreement

This agreement, when duly signed by both parties concerned, shall remain in force for 12 months from August 1, 2013 to July 31, 2014, and it shall be extended for another 12 months upon expiration unless notice in writing is given to the contrary.

14. Termination

During the validity of this agreement, if either of the two parties is found to have violated the stipulations herein, the other party has the right to terminate this agreement.

15. Force Majeure

Either party shall not be held responsible for failure or delay to perform all or any part of this agreement due to flood, fire, earthquake, draught, war or any other events which could not be predicted, controlled, avoided or overcome by the relative party. However, the party affected by the event of Force Majeure shall inform the other party of its occurrence in writing as soon as possible and thereafter send a certificate of the event issued by the relevant authorities to the other party within 15 days after its occurrence.

16. Arbitration

All disputes arising from the performance of this agreement shall be settled through friendly negotiation. Should no settlement be reached through negotiation, the case shall then be submitted for arbitration to the China International Economic and Trade Arbitration Commission (Beijing) and the rules of this Commission shall be applied. The award of the arbitration shall be final and binding upon both parties.

Party A:________ (Signature)

Party B:________ (Signature)

Notes

1. Singapore PSB certification: 新加坡 PSB 安全认证，其安全标志证书由新加坡安全主管当局（新加坡产品标准局）所核发。PSB 规定所有登记例管货物必须符合安全标准要求规格和普遍性安全的保证，从 1993 年 6 月 1 日起必须分别标示出安全标志。在新加坡负责销售例管货物给消费者的有关单位都必须向安全主管当局登记每个产品型号，登录时必须以证书和测试报告证实此型号符合强制性产品安全标准。

2. MD: Marketing Director，市场总监，销售主管，营销部主管。

Important Words and Phrases

1. furnace end　炉头
2. gas cooker　燃气灶
3. sole agent　独家代理（人）
4. exclusive agent　独家代理（人）
5. selling agent　销售代理
6. buying agent　购货代理
7. forwarding agent　运输代理
8. principal　委托方
9. express agency　明示代理
10. implied agency　默认代理
11. exclusivity agreement　独家经营/包销/代理协议
12. blanket order　总订单
13. letter of intent　意向书
14. exclusive privileges　独有的特权
15. monopolistic competition　垄断性竞争

16. terminate 终止
17. industrial property rights 工业产权
18. validity of agreement 代理期限
19. the parties concerned 当事人
20. Governmental Bodies 政府机构

Useful Expressions

1. You may rest assured that such a mistake will never occur again.
2. We think it premature for us to discuss the question of sole agency at the present stage.
3. We wish to inform you that this particular line has already been taken by ABC Company, who has acted as our sole agent for quite some time.
4. The question of sole agency is still under consideration and we hope that you will continue your efforts to push the sale of our products for the time being.
5. Your application for sole agency is now under our careful consideration.
6. We should be interested in acting as your sole agent.
7. We want to sign a sole agency agreement with you on this item for a period of 12 calendar months.
8. I've come again to renew our sole agency agreement for another 2 years.
9. Our agency agreement calls for a timely market report.
10. We hope you'll spare no efforts to promote the sale of our products so as to pave the way for renewing the sole agency agreement when it expires at the end of this year.
11. We can play an important part as a buying agent in your overseas trade.
12. Please get in touch with our sole agent for the supply of the goods you require.
13. We have to decline your proposal of acting as our sole agency in your area.
14. Unless you increase the turnover, we can hardly appoint you as our sole agent.
15. When opportunity matures, we will consider making you our exclusive agent in the U.S..
16. We'll consider appointing you as our sole agent for our food processers for the next two years in your local market.
17. How can we appoint you as our sole agent for such a small quantity?
18. I am here today to apply for the sole agency of your products in our local market.
19. It was two years ago that we made them our sole agent.
20. We've decided to entrust you with the sole agency for our dish-washing machines.

Exercises

1. Make a draft of Sole Agency Agreement according to the materials given below.

供应商: China National Import and Export Corporation
Chungshan Road, E. 1. Shanghai, China

代理商：James & Brothers Inc.

P. O. Box No.8

Sydney, Australia

代理产品：各种电动工具。

代理地区：澳大利亚悉尼市。

有效期: 2013 年 7 月 1 日～2014 年 6 月 30 日。

指标：所开立信用证的金额不少于 5 万美元。

付款条件：以即期信用证支付每一销售合同金额。

价格：代理商按供应商所报价格寄送订单给供应商，每笔交易以供应商销售合同最后确认为准。

2. 自选途径查阅一份一般代理协议，并将之翻译成中文。

3. 阅读并仿写以下代理函。

Dear Sirs,

For the past two years, we have been selling your disinfection cabinets to the wholesalers and big dealers located everywhere in Israel. Customers are quite satisfied with your products, as most of their specifications are suited to the markets. We have already set up a lot of solid business relations and have had excellent business performance.

Knowing that you gave no agent in Israel, we are, herewith, recommending ourselves as your agent. For your reference, we suggest to sign a sole agency agreement with 2 years' validity. The annual selling quantities will be at least 50 000 disinfection cabinets. We will take 15% commission from our concluded transactions. We will not run the other foreign similar and competitive products within the validity of this agreement.

If you agree to accept us as your sole agent, we will try our best to promote your products on the markets in Israel and make further study for this matter.

Your quick response will be highly appreciated.

Yours Faithfully,

×××

Appendix A Commonly Used Vocabulary in International Trade

国 际 贸 易

出口信贷	export credit
出口津贴	export subsidy
商品倾销	dumping
外汇倾销	exchange dumping
优惠关税	special preferences
保税仓库	bonded warehouse
贸易顺差	favorable balance of trade
贸易逆差	unfavorable balance of trade
进口配额制	import quotas
自由贸易区	free trade zone
对外贸易值	value of foreign trade
国际贸易值	value of international trade
普遍优惠制	generalized system of preferences（GSP）
最惠国待遇	most-favored nation treatment（MFNT）

价 格 条 件

价格条款	price term
运费	freight
单价	price
码头费	wharfage
总值	total value
卸货费	landing charges
金额	amount

关税	customs duty
净价	net price
印花税	stamp duty
含佣价	price including commission
港口税	port duty
回佣	return commission
装运港	port of shipment
卸货港	port of discharge
目的港	port of destination
折扣	discount/allowance
批发价	wholesale price
零售价	retail price
进口许可证	import license
出口许可证	export license
现货价格	spot price
期货价格	forward price
现行价格（时价）	current price /prevailing price
国际市场价格	world（international）market price
装运港船上交货价	free on board（FOB）
成本加运费价	cost and freight（C&F）
成本加运费、保险费价	cost, insurance and freight（CIF）

交 货 条 件

交货	delivery
轮船	steamship（S.S.）
装运、装船	shipment
租船	charter（the chartered ship）
定程租船	voyage charter
定期租船	time charter
交货时间	time of delivery
装运期限	time of shipment
托运人（一般指出口商）	shipper, consignor
收货人	consignee
班轮	regular shipping liner
驳船	lighter
舱位	shipping space

油轮	tanker
报关	clearance of goods
陆运收据	cargo receipt
空运提单	airway bill
正本提单	original B/L
提货	to take delivery of goods
选择港（任意港）	optional port
选港费	optional charges
选港费由买方负担	optional charges to be borne by the Buyers 或 optional charges for Buyers' account

1 月底装船 shipment not later than Jan.31st 或 shipment on or before Jan.31st

1/2 月份装船 shipment during Jan./Feb.或 Jan./Feb. shipment

在……（时间）分两批装船 shipment during...in two lots

在……（时间）平均分两批装船 shipment during...in two equal lots

分 3 个月装运 in three monthly shipments

分 3 个月，每月平均装运 in three equal monthly shipments

立即装运 immediate shipments

即期装运 prompt shipments

收到信用证后 30 天内装运 shipments within 30 days after receipt of L/C

不允许分批装船 partial shipment not allowed/not permitted

交易磋商、合同签订

订单	indent
订货，订购	book
电复	cable reply
实盘	firm offer
递盘	bid
递实盘	bid firm
还盘	counter offer
发盘（发价）	offer
发实盘	offer firm
询盘（询价）	inquiry（enquiry）
指示性（参考）价格	price indication/indicative price
速复	reply immediately
参考价	reference price
习惯做法	usual practice

交易磋商	business negotiation
不受约束	without engagement
业务洽谈	business discussion
限……复	subject to reply…
限……复到	subject to reply reaching here…
有效期限	time of validity
有效期至……	valid till…
购货合同	purchase contract
销售合同	sales contract
购货确认书	purchase confirmation
销售确认书	sales confirmation
一般交易条件	general terms and conditions
以未售出为准	subject to prior sale
需经卖方确认	subject to seller's confirmation
需经我方最后确认	subject to our final confirmation

贸易方式

拍卖	INT（auction）
寄售	consignment
招标	invitation of tender
投标	submission of tender
代理人	agent
代理协议	agency agreement
总代理人	general agent
独家代理	sole agency; sole agent; exclusive agency; exclusive agent
独家经营/专营权	exclusive right
独家经营/包销/代理协议	exclusivity agreement
累计佣金	accumulative commission
补偿贸易	compensation trade
来料加工	processing on giving materials/with supplied materials
来件装配	assembling on provided parts

品质条件

品质	quality
样品	sample

对等样品	counter sample
参考样品	reference sample
代表性样品	representative sample
封样	sealed sample
原样	original sample
复样	duplicate sample
规格	specifications
说明	description
标准	standard type
商品目录	catalogue
宣传小册	pamphlet
公差	tolerance
货号	article No.
花色（搭配）	assortment
增减 5% 5%	plus or minus
大路货（良好平均品质）	fair average quality（FAQ）

商 检 仲 裁

索赔	claim
争议	dispute
罚金	penalty
仲裁	arbitration
仲裁庭	arbitral tribunal
不可抗力	force majeure
产地证明书	certificate of origin
检验证书	inspection certificate
品质检验证书	inspection certificate of quality
重量（数量）检验证书	inspection certificate of weight（quantity）
商品检验局	commodity inspection bureau（CIB）

数 量 条 件

个数	number
净重	net weight
皮重	tare
毛重	gross weight

以毛作净	gross for net
容积	capacity
体积	volume
溢短装条款	more or less clause

外　汇

外汇	foreign exchange
外币	foreign currency
汇率	rate of exchange
浮动汇率	floating rate
买入汇率	buying rate
卖出汇率	selling rate
固定汇率	fixed rate
汇率波动的官定上下限	official upper and lower limits of fluctuation
通货膨胀	inflation
法定贬值	devaluation
法定升值	revaluation
国际收支	balance of payments
硬通货	hard currency
软通货	soft currency
直接标价	direct quotation
间接标价	indirect quotation
金本位	gold standard
金本位制度	gold standard system
黄金输送点	gold points
外汇平价	mint par
纸币制度	paper money system
国际货币基金	International Monetary Fund（IMF）
黄金外汇储备	gold and foreign exchange reserve

Appendix B

Major Ports of the World

港口/港口城市	所在国家
1. Abadan 阿巴丹	Iran 伊朗
2. Accra 阿克拉	Ghana 加纳
3. Aden 亚丁	Yemen 也门
4. Alexandria 亚历山大	Egypt 埃及
5. Algiers 阿尔及尔	Algeria 阿尔及利亚
6. Ambon 安汶	Indonesia 印度尼西亚
7. Amsterdam 阿姆斯特丹	Holland 荷兰
8. Antwerp 安特卫普	Belgium 比利时
9. Assab 阿萨布	The State of Eritrea 厄立特里亚
10. Auckland 奥克兰	New Zealand 新西兰
11. Bali 巴厘	Indonesia 印度尼西亚
12. Baltimore 巴尔的摩	U.S.A 美国
13. Bamako 巴马科	Mali 马里
14. Bandar Abbas 阿巴斯港	Iran 伊朗
15. Bangkok 曼谷	Thailand 泰国
16. Barcelona 巴塞罗纳	Spain 西班牙
17. Barranquilla 巴兰基亚	Colombia 哥伦比亚
18. Basra 巴士拉	Iraq 伊拉克
19. Beirut 贝鲁特	Lebanon 黎巴嫩
20. Belfast 贝尔法斯特	U.K.英国
21. Belize 伯利兹	Belize 伯利兹
22. Bergen 卑尔根	Norway 挪威
23. Bombay 孟买	India 印度
24. Bordeaux 波尔多	France 法国
25. Boston 波士顿	U.S.A.美国
26. Bremerhaven 不来梅港	Germany 德国

27. Brest 布雷斯特 France 法国
28. Brisbane 布里斯班 Australia 澳大利亚
29. Brussels 布鲁塞尔 Belgium 比利时
30. Buenos Aires 布宜诺斯艾利斯 Argentina 阿根廷
31. Busan/Pusan 釜山 R.O.K.韩国
32. Cagliari 卡利亚里 Italy 意大利
33. Cairo 开罗 Egypt 埃及
34. Calcutta 加尔各答 India 印度
35. Cape Town 开普敦 South Africa 南非
36. Cartagena 卡塔赫纳 Spain 西班牙
37. Casablanca 卡萨布兰卡 Morocco 摩洛哥
38. Chicago 芝加哥 U.S.A.美国
39. Chittagong 吉大港 Bangladesh 孟加拉国
40. Christchurch 克里斯特彻奇 New Zealand 新西兰
41. Chongjin 清津 D.P.R.K.朝鲜
42. Colombo 科伦坡 Sri Lanka 斯里兰卡
43. Concepcion 康塞普西翁 Chile 智利
44. Constanta 康斯坦察 Romania 罗马尼亚
45. Copenhagen 哥本哈根 Denmark 丹麦
46. Cork 科克 Ireland 爱尔兰
47. Dacca 达卡 Bangladesh 孟加拉国
48. Dalian 大连 China 中国
49. Denman 达曼 Saudi Arabia 沙特阿拉伯
50. Dandong 丹东 China 中国
51. Darwin 达尔文 Australia 澳大利亚
52. Dover 多佛尔 U.K.英国
53. Dubai 迪拜 U.A.E 阿联酋
54. Dublin 都柏林 Ireland 爱尔兰
55. Dunkirk 敦刻尔克 France 法国
56. Durban 德班 South Africa 南非
57. Durres 都拉斯 Albania 阿尔巴尼亚
58. Fuzhou 福州 China 中国
59. Gaoxiong 高雄 Taiwan, China 中国台湾省
60. Gdynia 格丁尼亚 Poland 波兰
61. Genoa 热那亚 Italy 意大利
62. Georgetown 乔治市 Malaysia 马来西亚
63. Good Hope 好望角 South Africa 南非

64. Gothenburg（Goteborg）哥德堡	Sweden 瑞典
65. Granville 格兰维尔	France 法国
66. Guangzhou 广州	China 中国
67. Guantanamo 关塔那摩	Cuba 古巴
68. Haikou 海口	China 中国
69. Halifax 哈利法克斯	Canada 加拿大
70. Hamburg 汉堡	Germany 德国
71. Havana 哈瓦那	Cuba 古巴
72. Helsingborg 赫尔辛堡	Sweden 瑞典
73. Helsinki 赫尔辛基	Finland 芬兰
74. Hiroshima 广岛	Japan 日本
75. Ho Chi Minh City（Saigon）胡志明市（西贡）	Vietnam 越南
76. Hong Kong 香港	China 中国
77. Houston 休斯顿	U.S.A.美国
78. Istanbul 伊斯坦布尔	Turkey 土耳其
79. Jakarta 雅加达	Indonesia 印度尼西亚
80. Java 爪哇	Indonesia 印度尼西亚
81. Jidda（Jeddah）吉达	Saudi Arabia 沙特阿拉伯
82. Karachi 卡拉奇	Pakistan 巴基斯坦
83. Kawasaki 川崎	Japan 日本
84. Khartoum 喀土穆	Sudan 苏丹
85. Kiel 基尔	Germany 德国
86. Kingston 金斯顿	Jamaica 牙买加
87. Kobe 神户	Japan 日本
88. Kuching 古晋	Malaysia 马来西亚
89. Kuwait 科威特	Kuwait 科威特
90. Kiev 基辅	Ukraine 乌克兰
91. La Guairá 拉瓜伊拉	Venezuela 委内瑞拉
92. La Paz 拉巴斯	Mexico 墨西哥
93. Le Havre 勒哈佛	France 法国
94. Lianyungang 连云港	China 中国
95. Limassol 利马索尔	Cyprus 塞浦路斯
96. Lisbon（Lisboa）里斯本	Portugal 葡萄牙
97. Liverpool 利物浦	U.K.英国
98. London 伦敦	U.K.英国
99. Long Beach 长滩	U.S.A.美国
100. Los Angeles 洛杉矶	U.S.A.美国

101. Luanda 罗安达	Angola 安哥拉
102. Macao 澳门	China 中国
103. Madras 马德拉斯	India 印度
104. Malacca（Melaka）马六甲	Malaysia 马来西亚
105. Malmo 马尔摩	Sweden 瑞典
106. Malta 马耳他	Malta 马耳他
107. Manchester 曼彻斯特	U.K.英国
108. Manila 马尼拉	Philippines 菲律宾
109. Maracaibo 马拉开波	Venezuela 委内瑞拉
110. Marseilles 马赛	France 法国
111. Melbourne 墨尔本	Australia 澳大利亚
112. Messina 墨西拿	Italy 意大利
113. Mombasa 蒙巴萨	Kenya 肯尼亚
114. Montreal 蒙特利尔	Canada 加拿大
115. Muscat 马斯喀特	Oman 阿曼
116. Nagasaki 长崎	Japan 日本
117. Nagoya 名古屋	Japan 日本
118. Nantes 南特	France 法国
119. Napier 纳皮尔	New Zealand 新西兰
120. Naples（Napoli）那不勒斯	Italy 意大利
121. Nelson 纳尔逊	New Zealand 新西兰
122. New Castle 纽卡斯尔	U.K.英国
123. New Orleans 新奥尔良	U.S.A.美国
124. New York 纽约	U.S.A.美国
125. Nice 尼斯	France 法国
126. Ningbo 宁波	China 中国
127. Odense 欧登塞	Denmark 丹麦
128. Oporto（Porto）波尔图	Portugal 葡萄牙
129. Oran 奥兰	Algeria 阿尔及利亚
130. Osaka 大阪	Japan 日本
131. Oslo 奥斯陆	Norway 挪威
132. Palembang 巨港	Indonesia 印度尼西亚
133. Panama City 巴拿马城	Panama 巴拿马
134. Penang 槟榔屿	Malaysia 马来西亚
135. Perth 佩斯	Australia 澳大利亚
136. Piraeus 比雷埃夫斯	Greece 希腊
137. Port Harcourt 哈尔科特港	Nigeria 尼日利亚

138. Port Kelang 巴生港	Malaysia 马来西亚
139. Port Louis 路易港	Mauritius 毛里求斯
140. Port Said 塞得港	Egypt 埃及
141. Port Sudan 苏丹港	Sudan 苏丹
142. Portland 波特兰	U.S.A.美国
143. Puerto Colombia 哥伦比亚港	Colombia 哥伦比亚
144. Qingdao 青岛	China 中国
145. Quebec 魁北克	Canada 加拿大
146. Rabat 拉巴特	Morocco 摩洛哥
147. Ravenna 拉文那	Italy 意大利
148. Reykjavik 雷克雅未克	Iceland 冰岛
149. Rijeka 里耶卡	Croatia 克罗地亚
150. Rio de Janeiro 里约热内卢	Brazil 巴西
151. Rosario 罗萨里奥	Argentina 阿根廷
152. Rostock 罗斯托克	Germany 德国
153. Rotterdam 鹿特丹	Holland 荷兰
154. Rouen 鲁昂	France 法国
155. Salonika 萨洛尼卡	Greece 希腊
156. Salvador 萨尔瓦多	Brazil 巴西
157. San Francisco 圣弗朗西斯科（旧金山）	U.S.A.美国
158. San Juan 圣胡安	Puerto Rico 波多黎各
159. Sandakan 山打根	Malaysia 马来西亚
160. San Diego 圣迭戈	U.S.A. 美国
161. Santos 圣多斯	Brazil 巴西
162. Sanya 三亚	China 中国
163. Seattle 西雅图	U.S.A.美国
164. Shanghai 上海	China 中国
165. Shekou 蛇口	China 中国
166. Singapore 新加坡	Singapore 新加坡
167. Southampton 南安普顿	U.K.英国
168. Stockholm 斯德哥尔摩	Sweden 瑞典
169. Subic 苏比克	Philippines 菲律宾
170. Suez Port 苏伊士港	Egypt 埃及
171. Sydney 悉尼	Australia 澳大利亚
172. Tamatave /Tamasina 塔马塔夫	Madagascar 马达加斯加
173. Tampico 坦皮科	Mexico 墨西哥
174. Tangier 丹吉尔	Morocco 摩洛哥

175. Tauranga 陶兰加 New Zealand 新西兰
176. Tel Aviv 特拉维夫 Israel 以色列
177. Tianjin Xingang 天津新港 China 中国
178. Timaru 提马鲁 New Zealand 新西兰
179. Tokyo 东京 Japan 日本
180. Toronto 多伦多 Canada 加拿大
181. Toulon 土伦 France 法国
182. Tunis 突尼斯 Tunis 突尼斯
183. Turku 图尔库 Finland 芬兰
184. Valencia 巴伦西亚 Spain 西班牙
185. Vancouver 温哥华 Canada 加拿大
186. Varna 瓦尔纳 Bulgaria 保加利亚
187. Venice 威尼斯 Italy 意大利
188. VeraCruz 维拉克鲁斯 Mexico 墨西哥
189. Victoria 维多利亚 Canada 加拿大
190. Vientiane 万象 Laos 老挝
191. Wellington 惠灵顿 New Zealand 新西兰
192. Wenzhou 温州 China 中国
193. Xiamen 厦门 China 中国
194. Yangon 仰光 Myanmar 缅甸
195. Yantai 烟台 China 中国
196. Yokohama 横滨 Japan 日本
197. Zanzibar 桑给巴尔 Tanzania 坦桑尼亚
198. Zhanjiang 湛江 China 中国

Appendix C Commonly Used Contracts and Agreements

上海市纺织品进出口公司
SHANGHAI TEXTILES IMPORT & EXPORT CORPORATION
27 ZHONGSHAN ROAD E.1, SHANGHAI, CHINA
TEL: 86-21-65342517 FAX: 86-21-65124743

编号
No. 21SSG-017

TO: CRYSTAL KOBE LTD.

售货确认书
SALES CONFIRMATION

日期
Date: AUG. 26, 2009

货号 ART. NO.	品名及规格 COMMODITY AND SPECIFICATION	数量 QUANTITY	单价及价格条款 UNIT PRICE &TERMS	金额 AMOUNT
H32331SE	LADIES' 55% ACRYLIC 45% COTTON KNITTED BLOUSE	120 CARTONS	USD 48.5 PER DOZ CIF C3 NEW YORK	USD24 250.00
			总金额 TOTAL AMOUNT	USD24 250.00

装运条款
SHIPMENT: SHIPMENT ON OR BEFORE NOV. 20, 2009 WITH PARTIAL SHIPMENTS NOT ALLOWED BUT TRANSSHIPMENT ALLOWED FROM SHANGHAI TO NEW YORK.

付款方式
PAYMENT: THE BUYER SHALL OPEN THROUGH A BANK ACCEPTABLE TO THE SELLER AN IRREVOCABLE L/C AT SIGHT TO REACH THE SELLER 30 DAYS BEFORE THE MONTH OF SHIPMENT REMAINED VALID FOR NEGOTIATION IN CHINA UNTIL THE 15TH DAY AFTER THE DATE OF SHIPMENT.

保 险
INSURANCE: THE SELLER SHALL COVER INSURANCE AGAINST ALL RISKS FOR 110 % OF THE TOTAL INVOICE VALUE AS PER THE RELEVANT OCEAN MARINE CARGO CLAUSE OF P.I.C.C. DATED JAN.1ST, 1981.

注 意：请完全按本售货确认书开证并在证内注明本售货确认书号码。
IMPORTANT: PLEASE ESTABLISH L/C EXACTLY ACCORDING TO THE TERMS AND CONDITIONS OF THIS S/C AND WITH THIS S/C NUMBER INDICATED.

____________________ SHANGHAI TEXTILES I/E CORPORATION

买方 （The Buyers） 卖方 （The Sellers）

上海市纺织品进出口公司
SHANGHAI TEXTILES IMPORT & EXPORT CORPORATION

CONTRACT

ORIGINAL

THE SELLER: SHANGHAI TEXTILES IMP. & EXP. CORP. CONTRACT NO.: GL0082
27 ZHONGSHAN ROAD E.1, SHANGHAI, CHINA DATE: Oct. 5, 2009
TEL: 86-21-65342517 FAX: 86-21-65124743 PLACE: SHANGHAI

THE BUYER: SUPERB AIM (HONG KONG) LTD.
RM.504 FUNG LEE COMM ERCIAL BLDG. 6-8A PRATT AVE., TSIMSHATSUI KOWLOO, HONG KONG

THE BUYER AND THE SELLER HAVE AGREED TO CONCLUDE THE FOLLOWING TRANSACTIONS ACCORDING TO THE TERMS AND CONDITIONS STIPULATED BELOW:

COMMODITY & SPECIFICATION	QUANTITY	UNIT PRICE(PCS)	AMOUNT
PACKING & SHIPPING MARK			
80% COTTON 20% POLYESTER LADIES, KNIT JACKET		CIF H.K.	
ART.NO.49394 (014428)	600PCS	USD14.25	USD 8 550.00
ART.NO.49393 (014428)	600PCS	USD14.25	USD 8 550.00
ART.NO.55306 (014429)	600PCS	USD14.25	USD 8 550.00
REMARKS:			TOTAL: USD 25 650.00
1) EACH IN PLASTIC BAGS, 24 BAGS TO A CARTON TOTAL: 75 CARTONS			
2) SHIPPING MARK: SUPERB H.K. NO.1-75 MADE IN CHINA			

TIME OF SHIPMENT: Within 45 days of receipt of letter of credit and not later than the month of Dec. 2009 with partial shipments and transshipment allowed.

PORT OF LOADING & DESTINATION: FROM SHANGHAI TO HONG KONG.

TERMS OF PAYMENT: By 100% Confirmed Irrevocable Sight Letter of Credit opened by the Buyer to reach the Seller not later than Oct. 31st, 2009 and to be available for negotiation in China until the 15th day after the date of shipment. In case of late arrival of the L/C, the Seller shall not be liable for any delay in shipment and shall have the right to rescind the contract and/or claim for damages.

INSURANCE: To be effected by the Seller for 110% of the CIF invoice value covering ALL RISKS and WAR RISK as per China Insurance Clauses.

TERMS OF SHIPMENT: To be governed by "INCOTERMS 2000". For transactions concluded on CIF terms, all surcharges including port congestion surcharges, etc. levied by the shipping company, in addition to freight, shall be for the Buyer's account.

The Buyer:
SUPERB AIM (HONG KONG) LTD.

The Seller:
SHANGHAI TEXTILES IMP.& EXP. CORP.

销售合同
SALES CONTRACT

卖方 **SELLER**	DESUN TRADING CO.,LTD. 29TH FLOOR KINGSTAR MANSION, 623 JINLIN RD. SHANGHAI, CHINA	编号 **NO.**	SHDS03027
		日期 **DATE**	APR.3, 2008
		地点 **SIGNED IN**	SHANGHAI
买方 **BUYER**	NEO GENERAL TRADING CO. #362 JALAN STREET, TORONTO, CANADA		

买卖双方同意按以下条款达成交易：
This contract is made by and agreed between the BUYER and the SELLER, in accordance with the terms and conditions stipulated below.

1. 品名及规格 **Commodity & Specification**	2. 数量 **Quantity**	3. 单价及价格条款 **Unit Price & Trade Terms**	4. 金额 **Amount**
			CIFC5 TORONTO
CHINESE CERAMIC DINNERWARE			
DS1511 30-Piece Dinnerware and Tea Set	542SETS	USD23.50	12 737.00
DS2201 20-Piece Dinnerware Set	800SETS	USD20.40	16 320.00
DS4504 45-Piece Dinnerware Set	443SETS	USD23.20	10 277.60
DS5120 95-Piece Dinnerware Set	254SETS	USD30.10	7 645.40
Total	**2 039SETS**		**46 980.00**

允许 10%溢短装，由卖方决定
With 10% more or less of shipment allowed at the seller's option

5. 总值 **Total Value**	SAY US DOLLARS FORTY SIX THOUSAND NINE HUNDRED AND EIGHTY ONLY.
6. 包装 **Packing**	DS2201 IN CARTONS OF 2 SETS EACH, DS1511, DS4504 AND DS5120 TO BE PACKED IN CARTONS OF 1 SET EACH ONLY. TOTAL: 1639 CARTONS.
7. 唛头 **Shipping Marks**	AT THE BUYER'S OPTION.
8. 装运期及运输方式 **Time of Shipment & Means of Transportation**	TO BE EFFECTED BEFORE THE END OF APRIL 2008 WITH PARTIAL SHIPMENT AND TRANSSHIPMENT ALLOWED.
9. 装运港及目的地 **Port of Loading & Destination**	FROM: SHANGHAI TO: TORONTO
10. 保险 **Insurance**	THE SELLER SHALL COVER INSURANCE AGAINST WPA AND CLASH & BREAKAGE & WAR RISKS FOR 110% OF THE TOTAL INVOICE VALUE AS PER THE RELEVANT OCEAN MARINE CARGO OF P.I.C.C. DATED 1/1/1981.
11. 付款方式 **Terms of Payment**	THE BUYER SHALL OPEN THROUGH A BANK ACCEPTABLE TO THE SELLER BEFORE APRIL 10, 2008 VALID FOR NEGOTIATION IN CHINA UNTIL THE 15TH DAY AFTER THE DATE OF SHIPMENT.
12. 备注 **Remarks**	

The Buyer	**The Seller**
NEO GENERAL TRADING CO.	DESUN TRADING CO.,LTD.
(signature)	(signature)

销售合同
SALES CONTRACT

合同号 Contract No.:
日期 Date:
签约地点 Signed At:

卖方 Sellers:
地址 Address:
买方 Buyers:
地址 Address:
兹买卖双方同意成交下列商品并订立条款如下：
The undersigned Sellers and Buyers have agreed to close the following transactions according to the terms and conditions stipulated below:

1. 货物名称及规格 Name of Commodity and Specification	2. 数量 Quantity	3. 单价 Unit Price	4. 金额 Amount	5. 总值 Total Value

数量及总值均得有____%的增减，由卖方决定。
With_____% more or less both in amount and quantity allowed at the Seller's option.
6. 包装：________________________________
Packing: ________________________________
7. 装运期限：□收到可以转船及分批装运之信用证___天内装出。
Time of Shipment: □Within___days after receipt of L/C allowing transshipment and partial shipment.
8. 装运口岸：______________________________
Port of Loading: ______________________________
9. 目的港：________________________________
Port of Destination: ____________________________
10. 付款条件：□开给我方100%不可撤销即期付款及可转让可分割之信用证，并须注明可在上述装运日期后15天内在中国议付有效。
Terms of Payment:□By 100% Confirmed, Irrevocable, Transferable and Divisible Letter of Credit to be available by sight draft and to remain valid for negotiation in China until the 15th day after the aforesaid Time of Shipment.
11. 保险：□按中国保险条款，保综合险及战争险（不包括罢工险）。
□由客户自理。
Insurance:□Covering All Risks and War Risk only (excluding S.R.C.C.) as per the China Insurance Clauses.
□To be effected by the buyers.

12. 装船标记：________________________________

Shipping Mark: ________________________________

13. 双方同意以装运港中国进出口商品检验局签发的品质和数量（重量）检验证书作为信用证项下议付所提交单据的一部分。买方有权对货物的品质和数量（重量）进行复验，复验费由买方负担。如发现品质和/或数量（重量）与合同不符，买方有权向卖方索赔。但须提供经卖方同意的公证机构出具之检验报告。

It is mutually agreed that the Inspection Certificate of Quality and Quantity (Weight) issued by the China Import and Export Commodity Inspection Bureau at the port of shipment shall be part of the documents to be presented for negotiation under the relevant L/C. The Buyers shall have the right to re-inspect the Quality and Quantity (Weight) of the cargo. The re-inspection fee shall be borne by the Buyers. Should the Quality and/or Quantity (Weight) be found not in conformity with that of the contract, the Buyers are entitled to lodge with the Sellers a claim which should be supported by survey reports issued by a recognized Surveyor approved by the Sellers.

14. 备注：

REMARKS:

（1）买方须于____年__月__日前开到本批交易的信用证（或通知卖方进口许可证号码），否则卖方有权不经通知取消本合同，或不接受买方对本约未执行的全部或一部，或对因此遭受的损失提出索赔。

The Buyers shall have the covering Letter of Credit reach the Sellers (or notify the Import License Number) before ________, otherwise the Sellers reserve the right to rescind without further notice or to accept whole or any part of this Sales Contract not fulfilled by the Buyers, or to lodge a claim for losses this sustained of any.

（2）凡以 CIF 条件成交的业务，保额为发票的 110%，投保险别以本销售合同中所开列的为限，若买方要求增加保额或保险范围，应于装船前经卖方同意，因此而增加的保险费由卖方负责。

For transactions concluded on C.I.F. basis it is understood that the insurance amount will be for 110% of the invoice value against the risks specified in the Sales Contract. If additional Insurance amount of coverage is required, the Buyers must have the consent of the Sellers before Shipment and the additional premium is to be borne by the Buyers.

（3）品质/数量异议：如买方提出索赔，凡属品质异议须于货到目的口岸之日起 3 个月内提出，凡属数量异议，须于货到目的口岸之日起 15 天内提出，对所装运物所提任何异议属于保险公司、轮船公司及其他有关运输机构或邮递机构所负责者，卖方不负任何责任。

QUALITY/QUANTITY DISCREPANCY: In case of quality discrepancy, claim should be filed by the Buyers within 3 months after the arrival of the goods at port of destination, while of quantity discrepancy, claim should be filed by the Buyers within 15 days after the arrival of the goods at port of destination. It is understood that the Sellers shall not be liable for any discrepancy of the goods shipped due to causes for which the Insurance Company, Shipping Company, other transportation, organization or post office are liable.

（4）本合同所述全部或部分商品，如因人力不可抗拒的原因，以致不能履约或延迟交货，卖方概不负责。

The Sellers shall not be held liable for failure or delay in delivery of the entire lot or a portion of the goods under this Sales Contract on consequence of any Force Majeure incidents.

（5）买方开给卖方的信用证上请填注本合同号码。

The Buyers are requested always to quote THE NUMBER OF THIS SALES CONTRACT in the Letter of Credit to be opened in favor of the Sellers.

（6）仲裁：凡因执行本合同或与本合同有关事项所发生的一切争执，应由双方通过友好的方式协商解决。如果不能取得协议，则在被告国家根据被告仲裁机构的仲裁程序规则进行仲裁。仲裁决定是终局的，对双方具有同等约束力。仲裁费用除非仲裁机构另有规定，均由败诉一方负担。

Arbitration: All disputes in connection with this Contract or the execution thereof shall be settled by negotiation between two parties. If no settlement can be reached, the case in dispute shall then be submitted for arbitration in the country of defendant in accordance with the arbitration regulations of the arbitration organization of the defendant country. The decision made by the arbitration organization shall be taken as final and binding upon both parties. The arbitration expenses shall be borne by the losing party unless otherwise awarded by the arbitration organization.

（7）买方收到本销售合同后立即签回一份，如买方对本合同有异议，应于收到后 5 天内提出，否则认为买方已同意本合同所规定的各项条款。

The Buyers are requested to sign and return one copy of this Sales Contract immediately after receipt of the same. Objection, if any, should be raised by the Buyers within five days after the receipt of this Sales Contract, in the absence of which it is understood that the Buyers have accepted the terms and conditions of the Sales Contract.

卖方	买方
THE SELLERS	THE BUYERS

AGREEMENT

Date:

This Agreement is made by and entered into between China National Import & Export Corporation (hereinafter referred to as Party A) and______________(hereinafter referred to as Party B), whereby Party A agrees to appoint Party B to act as its sole distributor for the under-mentioned commodity (ies) in the designated territory on the terms and conditions set forth below.

（1）Name of Commodity:

（2）Territory:

The territory covered by this Agreement is confined to _______ only. Party B shall exert its best efforts to push the sale of the specified commodity (ies) so as to secure the maximum volume of sales and shall not handle any of the specified commodity (ies) of other origins in the said territory. Party A agrees not to sell any of the specified commodity (ies) to other firms or importers in the said territory, except as provided in Article (8), and shall refer to Party B all inquiries received from clients in the said territory. However, if a third party insists on doing business direct with Party A, the latter shall have the right to do the business direct with the third party and allow Party B a 2% commission on the transaction.

（3）Price and Quantity

The price and quantity for the goods of each individual transaction are to be fixed through negotiations by both parties. Each transaction is subject to Party A's final conformation.

(4) Minimum Turnover

Party B undertakes to place with Party A orders amounting to _______ in the duration of this Agreement. The amount of the orders placed during the first three months shall not be less than 1/4 of the total amount as mentioned above.

(5) Payment

Payment is to be made by confirmed, irrevocable letter of credit, without recourse available by sight draft upon presentation of shipping documents to the negotiating bank in _____. The letter of credit for each order shall reach Party A ___ days before the date of shipment.

(6) Commission

Party A agrees to pay Party B a commission of ___% (___percent) on FOB value of orders placed by Party B under this Agreement. No commission shall be paid until Party A receives the full payment for each order.

(7) Tender

Party B undertakes to forward promptly to Party A all calls for tenders issued by local government bodies or their appointed representatives for the supply of the commodity (ies) covered by this Agreement together with all relevant information and/or materials. Should Party A decide to submit tender, offers shall be made through Party B with priority. The prices are to be mutually decided on each occasion. Party A, however, reserves the right to submit offers either directly or through a third party without being bound by this Agreement.

(8) Transactions with Governmental Bodies

The transactions concluded between Governmental bodies of Party A and Party B are not restricted by the terms and conditions of this Agreement, nor shall the amount of such transactions be counted as part of the turnover mentioned in this Agreement.

(9) Market Report

In order to keep Party A well informed of the prevailing market conditions, Party B shall undertake to supply Party A, at least one calendar quarter or at any time when necessary, with a market report covering information on changes of local regulations in connection with the importation and sales of the commodity (ies) covered by this Agreement, local market tendency, and buyers' comments on quality, packing, price, etc. of the goods supplied by Party A under this Agreement. Party B shall also supply Party A with quotations, samples and advertising matters of similar commodity (ies) of other suppliers.

(10) Validity of the Agreement

This Agreement is to remain valid for a period of ___ commencing from _______________ and terminating on _______. If either party considers it necessary to extend the Agreement, the proposing party may take the initiative to conduct negotiation with the other party one month prior to its expiration.

(11) In the event of a breach of any of the provision of this Agreement by one party, the

other party may at its option cancel this Agreement forthwith by giving notice in writing to the defaulting party.

Party A Party B

Joint Venture Contract

This Contract is made on the___day of___, 20___between Shanghai Building Materials Import&Export Corporation organized under the laws of the People's Republic of China, having its principal office at __________ Shanghai, the People's Republic of China (hereinafter called Party A) of the First Part, and The Global Construction Supplies Company organized under the laws of the USA, having its principal office at __________ Ohio, USA (hereinafter called Party B) of the Second Part.

Recitals

WHEREAS Party A desires to use Party B's Technology and Trademark to manufacture and sell Road Marks in China and overseas markets;

WHEREAS Party B desires to cooperate with Party A to manufacture and sell Road Marks in China and overseas markets; and

WHEREAS both parties consider these objectives can best be achieved by the formation of a joint venture company under the relevant laws, rules and regulations of the People's Republic of China.

NOW THEREFORE, in consideration of the premises and the covenants described hereinafter, Party A and Party B agree as follows:

Article 1 ESTABLISHMENT OF THE JOINT VENTURE COMPANY

1.1 In accordance with the Laws of the People's Republic of China on Joint Venture Using Chinese and Foreign Investment and other relevant Chinese laws and regulations, both parties agree to set up a joint venture limited liability company (hereinafter called the joint venture company).

1.2 The Chinese name of the joint venture company, as agreed upon, is 高速公路建筑材料供应公司.

1.3 The English name of the joint venture company, as agreed upon, is Superhighway Construction Supplier Company (abbreviated as SCSC).

1.4 The principal office of SCSC and its registered address is __________ Shanghai, the People's Republic of China.

1.5 The organization form of the joint venture company is a limited liability company.
Each party to the joint venture company is liable to the joint venture company within the

limit of the capital subscribed by it. The profits, risks and losses of the joint venture company shall be shared by the parties in proportion to their contributions of the registered capital.

1.6 The expenses of incorporation shall be shared equally between Party A and Party B.

1.7 All activities of the joint venture company shall be governed by the laws, decrees and pertinent rules and regulations of the People's Republic of China.

Article 2 PURPOSE, SCOPE AND SCALE OF PRODUCTION AND BUSINESS

2.1 The purpose of the parties to the joint venture is in conformity with the wish of enhancing the economic cooperation and technical exchanges, improving the product quality, developing new products, appropriate technology and scientific management so as to raise economic results and ensure satisfactory economic benefits.

2.2 The productive and business scope of the joint venture company is to manufacture Road Marks, provide instructions and directions for construction, collect quality data from practical use for research and improvement.

2.3 The productive and business scope of the joint venture company put into operation is ________________.

In the second 12 months when the company parts are produced by the joint venture company itself, the production capacity is ________________.

With the development of production and successful operation, the variety of product may be increased to___kinds.

Article 3 REGISTERED CAPITAL

3.1 The registered capital of the joint venture company is Renminbi____________Yuan (equivalent to US$ __________), which will be contributed by Party A and Party B equally.

Party A's contribution

Cash______________________Yuan

Land use right________________Yuan

Premises____________________Yuan (to be evaluated by joint group)

Machines and equipment_______Yuan (ditto)

Others______________________Yuan (ditto)

Total_______________________Yuan (accounting for 50% of the registered capital)

Party B's contribution

Cash______________________Yuan (to be converted from US dollars according to the exchange rate on the date this Contract becomes effective)

Technology (including technical data, know-how and trademark)___________ Yuan (to be evaluated by joint group)
Component parts supplied in the first 12 months______________________Yuan (ditto)
Total______________________Yuan (accounting for 50% of the registered capital)

3.2 The total investment shall be fully made within 12 calendar months commencing from the date on which the business licence is issued to and obtained by the joint venture company. To facilitate construction of the factory premises, an initial investment is to be made in cash by Party A and Party B each amounting to Renminbi___________Yuan, which shall be paid within one month after the incorporation of the joint venture company (i.e. after the business licence is issued and obtained).The balance of the investment including the evaluation of property and the right to the use of land, etc. should be fulfilled within the aforementioned 12 calendar months.

3.3 In case any party to the joint venture intends to assign all or part of its investment subscribed to a third party, consent shall be obtained from the other party to the joint venture, and approval from the examination and approval authorities is required. When one party to the joint venture assigns all or part of its investment, the other party shall have the preemptive right to purchase.

Article 4 BOARD OF DIRECTORS

4.1 The date of registration of the joint venture company shall be the date of the establishment of the Board of Directors of the joint venture company.

4.2 The Board of Directors are composed of six directors of which three shall be appointed by Party A and three by Party B. The chairman of the Board shall be appointed by Party A, and its vice chairman by Party B. The term of office for the directors, chairman and vice chairman is four years. Their terms of office may be renewed if continuously appointed by the relevant party.

4.3 The highest authority of the joint venture company shall be its Board of Directors. It shall decide all major issues concerning the joint venture company. Unanimous approval shall be required before any decisions are made on major issues. As for other matters, approval by majority or a simple majority shall be required.

4.4 The chairman of the Board is the legal representative of the joint venture company. Should the chairman be unable to exercise his or her responsibilities for some reasons, he or she shall authorize the vice chairman or any other directors to represent the joint venture company temporarily.

4.5 The Board of Directors shall convene at least one meeting every year. The meeting shall be called and presided over the chairman of the Board. The chairman may convene an interim meeting based on a proposal made by one third of the total members of directors. Minutes of meeting shall be placed on file.

Article 5 BUSINESS MANAGEMENT OFFICE

5.1 The joint venture company shall establish a management office which shall be responsible for its daily management. It shall have a general manager, appointed by Party A, and a deputy general manager, appointed by Party B. Their terms of office are four years.

5.2 The responsibility of the general manager is to carry out the decisions of the Board of Directors and organize and conduct the routine work of the joint venture company. The deputy general manager shall assist the general manager in his or her work.

5.3 In case of graft or serious dereliction of duty on the part of the general manager and/or the deputy general manager, the Board of Directors shall have the power to dismiss them at any time.

Article 6 RESPONSIBILITIES OF PARTIES

Responsibilities of Party A

6.1 to apply for and obtain the business licence, to make tax registration and obtain all possible tax reductions and exemptions according to the laws of the People's Republic of China;

6.2 to organize construction of the factory premises, to install machinery and equipment, to settle the fundamental facilities, such as water, electricity, communication and transportation etc.;

6.3 to obtain necessary entry visas for foreign staff and workers and provide convenience for their traveling on business in China;

6.4 to recruit Chinese staff, engineers, technicians, workers and translators;

6.5 to apply to the Bank of China or any other banks approved by the State Administration of Exchange Control for the opening of foreign currency and Renminbi accounts.

Responsibilities of Party B

6.6 to expedite shipment of machinery, equipment and component parts; to provide technology and send technical personnel for installing, testing and inspecting;

6.7 to train Chinese technical personnel and workers at Party B's plants and/or other locations agreeable to both parties according to the training programs duly agreed upon;

6.8 to solve problems concerning technology, operation and management which may arise in the course of production;

6.9 to collect appropriate scientific and technological information, as well as economic and legal information that may be of use to the normal operation of the joint venture company.

Article 7 PURCHASE OF NEEDFUL MATERIALS

7.1 In purchase of required raw materials, fuel, parts, means of transportation and articles for office use, the joint venture company shall give first priority to purchase in China where conditions are the same.

7.2 In case the joint venture company entrusts Party B to make purchases on overseas markets, persons appointed by Party A shall be invited to take part in the purchasing.

Article 8 SALE OF PRODUCTS

8.1 The products of the joint venture company shall be sold both on Chinese market and on overseas market. The export part accounts for 50%, whereas the other 50% is for domestic market. Party B shall be responsible for the sale of the products abroad.

8.2 The joint venture company may directly sell its products on the international market. It may also sign sales contracts with Chinese or foreign trade companies, entrusting them to be its sales agents.

8.3 The joint venture company may set up sales branches both in China and abroad subject to the approval of the relevant Chinese Department. The function of the sales branches, besides sales, is to collect users' comments on product quality and give instructions for the correct use of the products.

Article 9 LABOUR MANAGEMENT

9.1 Labour contracts covering employment, dismissal and resignation of the staff and workers of the joint venture company, and their production tasks, wages, awards and punishment, holidays and paid leaves of absence, labour insurance and welfare benefits, labour protection, labour discipline and other matters shall be signed between the joint venture company and its staff.

9.2 The labour contract duly signed shall be filed with the local labour management authorities.

9.3 The appointment of high-ranking administrative personnel recommended by both parties, their salaries, social insurance, welfare and the standard of travelling expenses, etc. shall be decided by the Board of Directors.

Article 10 TAXES, FINANCE AND AUDIT

10.1 The joint venture company shall pay taxes in accordance with the stipulations of Chinese laws and other relevant regulations.

10.2 Staff and workers of the joint venture company shall pay individual income tax according to the "Individual Income Tax Law of the People's Republic of China".

10.3 The joint venture company shall establish its accounting system in accordance with the relevant regulations for financial accounting in China.

10.4 The fiscal year of the joint venture company shall be from January 1 to December 31. All vouches, receipts, statistic statements and reports, account books shall be written in Chinese. English may be used concurrently with mutual consent.

10.5 Financial checking and examination of the joint venture company shall be conducted by an auditor registered in China. Reports shall be submitted to the Board of Directors and the general manager.

10.6 The manager of the joint venture company shall, within 30 days after the end of its fiscal year, prepare an annual financial statement to be submitted to the Board of Directors for examination and approval. The financial statement shall include a balance sheet, profit and loss statement audited and certified as true and correct by an auditor registered in China.

Article 11 DURATION OF THE JOINT VENTURE

The duration of the joint venture company is TEN years commencing from the date on which the business licence of the joint venture company is issued. It may be extended for FIVE years upon mutual consent. The application for the extension of the duration shall be submitted to the examination and approval authority SIX months prior to the expiry date of the joint venture company.

Article 12 TERMINATION AND LIQUIDATION

12.1 In case of inability to fulfill the contract or to continue operation due to heavy losses in successive years as a result of force majeure, the duration of the joint venture contract shall be terminated before its expiration after unanimously agreed upon by the Board of Directors and approved by the original examination and approval authority.

12.2 Should the joint venture company be unable to continue its operation or achieve the business purposes stipulated in the contract on account of the fact that one of the contracting parties fails to fulfill its obligation or seriously violates the stipulations of the contract and articles of association, the other party shall have the right to terminate the contract. The termination shall be approved by the original examination and approval authority.

12.3 Liquidation and the distribution of the liquidated assets shall be carried out in accordance with the contract stipulations and the relevant laws and regulations of the People's Republic of China.

Article 13 ASSIGNMENT

Assignment may be made if it is agreed upon by both parties as stipulated in Art. 3.3.

However, it (the assignment) shall neither interrupt the normal operation nor affect the organization structure of the joint venture company during the process of assignment.

Article 14　INSURANCE

During the term of this contract the joint venture company shall affect insurance against various risks preferably with the People's Insurance Company of China, which handles claims promptly and equitably.

Article 15　FORCE MAJEURE

Should either party be prevented from executing the contract owing to an event of force majeure, such as earthquake, typhoon, flood, fire, explosion, war, insurrection, epidemic and quarantine restriction, the prevented party shall immediately notify the other party by telex or fax, and within 15 days thereafter provide a certificate issued by the relevant government authorities confirming such force majeure and explaining the reason for its inability to execute or delay the execution of all or part of this contract. Both parties shall therefore, through friendly consultations, decide whether to terminate the contract before its expiration or to delay executing all or part of this contract or to exempt part of the contract obligations for implementation according to the effects of the event. If decision is made to continue the contract, the time for execution shall be extended by a period equal to period of the delay caused by such force majeure.

Article 16　AMENDMENT AND ALTERATION

Amendment to and alteration of this contract or its appendices shall become effective only after a written agreement signed by both parties and approved by the original examination and approval authority.

Article 17　SETTLEMENT OF DISPUTES

Any disputes arising from the execution of or in connection with the contract shall be settled through friendly consultations between the two parties. In case such consultations fail to settle the disputes, then the disputes shall be submitted for arbitration. In China, the arbitration shall be conducted by the Foreign Economic & Trade Arbitration Commission of the China Council for the Promotion of International Trade in accordance with its rules of procedure, or the arbitration shall take place in a third country agreed upon by both parties in accordance with the rules of procedure of that country.

Article 18 APPLICABLE LAW

The formation of this contract, its validity, interpretation, execution and settlement of disputes shall be governed by the relevant laws and regulations of the People's Republic of China.

Article 19 LANGUAGE

The contract shall be written in Chinese version and in English version. Both versions are equally authentic. In the event of any discrepancy between the two aforementioned versions, the Chinese version shall prevail.

IN WITNESS WHEREOF, the parties have executed this contract in quadruplicate by their duly authorized representatives as of the date first above written.

Shanghai Building Materials	The Global Construction
Import & Export Corp.	Supplies Company
Director	Director

Compensation Trade Agreement

This agreement is made on the___day of___, 20___,

Between

Shing Hua Gum Products Mfg. Co., Shanghai, China (hereinafter called Party A) of the First Part,

And

Swiss Industrial Products Suppliers Ltd., Zurich, Switzerland (hereinafter called Party B) of the Second Part,

whereby the two parties, through friendly negotiation, agree to conclude the following compensation trade agreement on the terms and conditions set forth below:

1) Party A agrees to import from Party B a complete set of GM-92 machine to revamp its production, the details of which are shown in Appendix No.1.

2) Party B agrees to sell a complete set of GM-92 machine to Party A as per details shown in Appendix No.1. Party B guarantees that the machine supplied for sale is brand new and in perfect condition. If any defect occurs in the performance of the machine, Party A shall have the right to file a claim against Party B for any loss or losses sustained by Party A.

3) As agreed upon by both parties, the total cost of the machine including freight, insurance, installation and testing is US$ 900 000, namely

Machine including components	US $ 840 000
Freight including inland transportation, etc.	US $ 42 100

Insurance covering All Risks & War Risk	US $ 5 400
Installation & Testing	US $ 12 500
	US $900 000

If freight, insurance and/or installation charges etc. exceed the above-mentioned figures, the exceeding amount shall be for Party B's account. In other words, the total amount of purchase is US$ 900 000, and the machine is to be delivered to the factory premise designated by Party A and properly installed.

4) Party A shall supply Party B for export with the products produced with the imported machine or, if necessary, with the products produced or provided by other suppliers to offset the total cost of the imported machine.

5) Party B agrees that the cost of the machine shall be repaid by Party A with the products produced with the imported machine or with products provided by other suppliers on condition that such products meet with Party B's requirements.

6) As agreed upon by both parties, repayment of the cost of the imported machine shall be fulfilled in two years commencing from the day on which testing proves that the machine is in perfect working condition and a testing certificate is issued by the competent authorities.

7) Upon receipt of the testing certificate, Party A shall pay Party B a down payment of US $100 000 through the Bank of China, Shanghai and at the same time requests the said bank to issue a letter of guarantee in favor of Party B ensuring punctual delivery of the buyback products to offset the outstanding amount of the cost of the imported machine as prescribed in Article 5 of this agreement.

8) Repayments shall be made by quarterly installments, namely, US$ 100 000 each quarter, and for the sake of convenience, reciprocal letters of credit are to be opened simultaneously by Party A and Party B with their own bank one month prior to the estimated date of shipment of the buyback products.

9) Party B guarantees to place orders with Party A every three months for the buyback products amounting to US$100 000 (approximately). For orders received and booked, Party A shall send sales contracts in duplicate to Party B. The duplicate copies of the sales contracts shall be counter-signed by Party B and returned to Party A for file. It is agreed that in executing orders Party A shall give priority to the orders received from Party B.

10) In case Party B fails to place orders to the amount stipulated in Article 9 of this agreement, the short amount shall be carried forward to the next quarter to be fulfilled by Party B.

11) In case Party B fails to open the reciprocal L/C for the orders placed, Party A shall have

the right to sell the products to any other buyer and debit Party B's account with the storage charges and losses arising from Party B's non-fulfillment of its obligation as set forth in Article 9 of this agreement.

12) In case Party B places orders exceeding the amount required for quarterly repayment, Party A, if possible, shall accept and execute the orders; however,

① if the exceeding amount is small, it shall be carried forward to the following quarter to offset the amount of repayment;

② if the exceeding amount is large, it shall be regarded as the amount of a separate transaction, for which Party B is requested to open a covering L/C.

13) Should Party A be unable to supply the buyback products during the regulated period of three months, Party B shall have the right to ask the Bank of China to make the necessary repayment under the letter of guarantee by giving details of evidence showing Party A's inability to perform its obligation.

14) Payments by Party A for the imported machine and payments by Party B for the buyback products shall be accounted for separately and offset each other. At the end of the 4th quarter, i.e. after a period of 12 calendar months, Party A shall provide a statement of accounts, which is to be checked and verified by a registered auditor. Should any differences appear in the two accounts, Party A and Party B shall conduct negotiations and make a plan to balance the accounts.

15) Should either party be prevented from performing any of its obligations under this agreement owing to an event of force majeure, the time for performance under this agreement shall be extended. The period to be extended shall be discussed and decided between and by the two parties. The prevented party shall notify the other party by telex or telephone as soon as an event of force majeure occurs. It shall also provide a certificate from the relevant government authorities confirming such force majeure and stating the reason of its inability to perform its obligations.

16) After the imported machine has been installed and put to use, Party B shall send technicians at its own expense to train Party A's workers to operate and maintain the machine. The time required as agreed upon by both parties is three months. Party A shall offer free accommodations for Party B's personnel during their stay in Shanghai as return for Party B's after-sales service.

17) Any differences in opinion and/or disputes in connection with this agreement or the execution thereof shall be settled amicably through friendly negotiation.

18) This agreement is written in Chinese and English versions. Both versions are equally authentic. In the event of any discrepancy between the two aforesaid versions, the Chinese version shall prevail. IN WITNESS WHEREOF, the parties have executed this agreement in quadruplicate by their duly authorized representatives as of the date first

above written.

Party A	Party B
Shing Hua Gum Products Mfg. Co.	Swiss Industrial Products
Shanghai, China	Suppliers Ltd.
	Zurich, Switzerland
Signed.	Signed.

Appendix D

Relative Documents and Credits

中国纺织品进出口公司上海市分公司

CHINA NATIONAL TEXTILES IMPORT & EXPORT CORPORATION

SHANGHAI BRANCH

27 Zhongshan Road E.1, Shanghai, China

TEL: 86-21-65342517 FAX: 86-21-65124743

报 价 单

QUOTATION

致

Messrs.: CRYSTAL KOBE LTD.

日期

Dated: AUG. 8, 2009

兹报供下列商品，均以我方最后确认为准。

The following articles are quoted subject to our final confirmation:

货号 ART. NO.	品名 COMMODITY	规格 SPECIFICATIONS	包装 PACKING	单价 UNIT PRICE	装船期 SHIPMENT
H32331SE	LADIES' BLOUSE	55%ACRYLIC 45% COTTON KNITTED	IN CARTONS	USD 50.00 PER DOZ	CIF NY ON/OR BEFORE DEC. 20, 2009

付款方式

PAYMENT: BY L/C AT SIGHT

保险

INSURANCE：For 110% OF TOTAL INVOICE VALUE COVERING ALL RISKS

信用证 1

<table>
<tr><td colspan="5">THE ROYAL BANK OF CANADA
BRITISH COLUMBIA INTERNATIONAL CENTRE
1055 WEST GEORGIA STREET, VANCOUVER, B.C. V6E 3P3
CANADA</td></tr>
<tr><td colspan="3">□CONFIRMATION OF TELEX/CABLE PER-ADVISED
TELEX NO. 4720688 CA</td><td colspan="2">DATE: APR. 8, 2008
PLACE:VANCOUVER</td></tr>
<tr><td colspan="2">IRREVOCABLE DOCUMENTARY CREDIT</td><td>CREDIT NUMBER: 01/0501-FCT</td><td colspan="2">ADVISING BANK'S REF. NO.</td></tr>
<tr><td colspan="2">**ADVISING BANK:**
SHANGHAI AJ FINANCE CORPORATION
#59 HONGKONG ROAD
SHANGHAI 200002, CHINA</td><td colspan="3">**APPLICANT:**
NEO GENERAL TRADING CO.
#362 JALAN STREET, TORONTO, CANADA</td></tr>
<tr><td colspan="2">**BENEFICIARY:**
DESUN TRADING CO., LTD.
29TH FLOOR KINGSTAR MANSION,
623JINLIN RD., SHANGHAI CHINA</td><td colspan="3">**AMOUNT:**
USD46 980.00
(US DOLLARS FORTY SIX THOUSAND NINE HUNDRED AND EIGHTY ONLY)</td></tr>
<tr><td colspan="2">**EXPIRY DATE:** MAY 15, 2008</td><td colspan="3">FOR NEGOTIATION IN CHINA / BENEFICIARY COUNTRY</td></tr>
<tr><td colspan="5">**GENTLEMEN:**
WE HEREBY OPEN OUR IRREVOCABLE LETTER OF CREDIT IN YOUR FAVOR WHICH IS AVAILABLE BY YOUR DRAFTS AT SIGHT FOR FULL INVOICE VALUE ON US ACCOMPANIED BY THE FOLLOWING **DOCUMENTS:**
+SIGNED COMMERCIAL INVOICE AND 3 COPIES.
+PACKING LIST AND 3 COPIES, SHOWING THE INDIVIDUAL WEIGHT AND MEASUREMENT OF EACH ITEM.
+ORIGINAL CERTIFICATE OF ORIGIN AND 3 COPIES ISSUED BY THE CHAMBER OF COMMERCE.
+FULL SET CLEAN ON BOARD OCEAN BILLS OF LADING MARKED “FREIGHT PREPAID” CONSIGNED TO ORDER OF THE ROYAL BANK OF CANADA INDICATING THE ACTUAL DATE OF THE GOODS ON BOARD AND NOTIFY THE APPLICANT WITH FULL ADDRESS AND PHONE NO. 77009910.
+INSURANCE POLICY OR CERTIFICATE FOR 110 PERCENT CIF OF INVOICE VALUE COVERING WPA AND CLASH & BREAKAGE & WAR RISK AS PER THE RELEVANT OCEAN MARINE CARGO OF P.I.C.C. DATED 1/1/1981.
+BENEFICIARY'S CERTIFICATE CERTIFYING THAT EACH COPY OF SHIPPING DOCUMENTS HAS BEEN FAXED TO THE APPLICANT WITHIN 48 HOURS AFTER SHIPMENT.
COVERING SHIPMENTS:
4 ITEMS OF CHINESE CERAMIC DINNERWARE INCLUDING:
DS1511 30-PIECE DINNERWARE AND TEA SET, 542 SETS
DS2201 20-PIECE DINNERWARE SET, 800 SETS
DS4504 45-PIECE DINNERWARE SET, 443 SETS
DS5120 95-PIECE DINNERWARE SET, 254 SETS
DETAILS IN ACCORDANCE WITH SALES CONTRACT SHDS03027 DATED APR. 3, 2008.
[ ] FOB / [ ] CFR / [X] CIF/ [ ] FAX TORONTO CANADA.</td></tr>
<tr><td>**SHIPMENT FROM**
SHANGHAI</td><td>**TO**
TORONTO</td><td>**LATEST**
APRIL 30, 2008</td><td>**PARTIAL SHIPMENTS**
ALLOWED</td><td>**TRANSSHIPMENT**
ALLOWED</td></tr>
<tr><td colspan="5">DRAFTS TO BE PRESENTED FOR NEGOTIATION WITHIN 15 DAYS AFTER THE DATE OF SHIPMENT BUT WITHIN THE VALIDITY OF CREDIT. ALL DOCUMENTS TO BE FORWARDED IN ONE COVER, BY AIRMAIL, UNLESS OTHERWISE STATED UNDER SPECIAL INSTRUCTION.</td></tr>
<tr><td colspan="5">SPECIAL INSTRUCTION: ALL BANKING CHARGES OUTSIDE CANADA ARE FOR ACCOUNT OF BENEFICIARY.
+ALL GOODS MUST BE SHIPPED IN FOUR 20'CY TO CY CONTAINERS AND B/L SHOWING THE SAME.
+THE VALUE OF FREIGHT PREPAID HAS TO BE SHOWN ON BILLS OF LADING.
+DOCUMENTS WHICH FAIL TO COMPLY WITH THE TERMS AND CONDITIONS IN THE LETTER OF CREDIT SUBJECT TO A SPECIAL DISCREPANCY HANDLING FEE OF US$35.00 TO BE DEDUCTED FROM ANY PROCEEDS.</td></tr>
<tr><td colspan="5">DRAFT MUST BE MARKED AS BEING DRAWN UNDER THIS CREDIT AND BEAR ITS NUMBER; THE AMOUNTS ARE TO BE ENDORSED ON THE REVERSE HEREOF BY NEG. BANK. WE HEREBY AGREE WITH THE DRAWERS, ENDORSERS AND FIDE HOLDER THAT ALL DRAFTS DRAWN UNDER AND IN COMPLIANCE WITH THE TERMS OF THIS CREDIT SHALL BE DULY HONORED UPON PRESENTATION.
THIS CREDIT IS SUBJECT TO THE UNIFORM CUSTOMS AND PRACTICE FOR DOCUMENTARY CREDITS (1993 REVISION) BY THE INTERNATIONAL CHAMBER OF COMMERCE PUBLICATION NO. 600.</td></tr>
<tr><td colspan="2">David Jone</td><td colspan="3">Yours Very Truly,
Joanne Hsan</td></tr>
<tr><td colspan="2">AUTHORIZED SIGNATURE</td><td colspan="3">AUTHORIZED SIGNATURE</td></tr>
</table>

信用证 2

2009MAR. 22 09:18:11 MT S700		ISSUE OF A DOCUMENTARY CREDIT PAGE 00001	LOGICAL TERMINAL E102 FUN CMSG700 UMR 06881051
MSGACK DWS765I AUTH OK, KEY B198081689580FC5, BKCHCNBJ RJHISARI RECORD			
BASIC HEADER		F 01 BKCHCNBJA940 0588 550628	
APPLICATION HEADER		0 700 1057 010320 RJHISARIAXXX 7277 977367 020213 1557 N *ALRAJHI BANKING AND INVESTMENT *CORPORATION *RIYADH *(HEAD OFFICE)	
USER HEADER		SERVICE CODE 103 （银行盖信用证通知专用章） BANK PRIORITY 113 MSG USER REF. 108 INFO. FROM CI 115	
SEQUENCE OF TOTAL	*27	1 / 1	
FORM OF DOC. CREDIT	*40 A	IRREVOCABLE	
DOC. CREDIT NUMBER	*20	0011LC123756	
DATE OF ISSUE	31 C	090320	
DATE/PLACE EXP.	*31D	**DATE 0905015 PLACE CHINA**	
APPLICANT	*50	NEO GENERAL TRADING CO. P.O. BOX 99552, RIYADH 22766, KSA TEL: 00966-1-84659220 FAX: 00966-1-84659213	
BENEFICIARY	*59	DESUN TRADING CO., LTD. HUARONG MANSION RM2901 NO.85 GUANJIAQIAO, NANJING 210005, CHINA TEL: 0086-25-4715004 FAX: 0086-25-4711363	
AMOUNT	*32 B	CURRENCY USD AMOUNT 13 260.00	
AVAILABLE WITH/BY	*41 D	ANY BANK IN CHINA, BY NEGOTIATION	
DRAFTS AT ...	42 C	SIGHT	
DRAWEE	42 A	RJHISARI	
		*ALRAJHI BANKING AND INVESTMENT *CORPORATION *RIYADH *(HEAD OFFICE)	
PARTIAL SHIPMENT	43 P	NOT ALLOWED	
TRANSSHIPMENT	43 T	NOT ALLOWED	
LOADING ON BRD.	44 A	SHANGHAI PORT, CHINA	
	44 B	DAMMAM PORT, SAUDI ARABIA	
LATEST SHIPMENT	44 C	010430	
GOODS DESCRIPT	45 A	ABOUT 1700 CARTONS CANNED MUSHROOM PIECES & STEMS 24 TINS ×425 GRAMS NET WEIGHT (D.W. 227 GRAMS) AT USD 7.80 PER CARTON, ROSE BRAND.	

Continue

DOCS. REQUIRED	46 A	DOCUMENTS REQUIRED
		+ SIGNED COMMERCIAL INVOICE IN TRIPLICATE ORIGINAL AND MUST SHOW BREAK DOWN OF THE AMOUNT AS FOLLOWS: FOB VALUE, FREIGHT CHARGES AND TOTAL AMOUNT C AND F.
		+ FULL SET CLEAN ON BOARD BILL OF LADING MADE OUT TO THE ORDER OF ALRAJHI BANKING AND INVESTMENT CORP., MARKED FREIGHT PREPAID AND NOTIFY APPLICANT, INDICATING THE FULL NAME, ADDRESS AND TEL NO. OF THE CARRYING VESSEL'S AGENT AT THE PORT OF DISCHARGE.
		+ PACKING LIST IN ONE ORIGINAL PLUS 5 COPIES, ALL OF WHICH MUST BE MANUALLY SIGNED.
		+ INSPECTION (HEALTH) CERTIFICATE FROM C.I.Q. (ENTRY-EXIT INSPECTION AND QUARANTINE OF THE PEOPLE'S REP. OF CHINA) STATING GOODS ARE FIT FOR HUMAN BEING.
		+ CERTIFICATE OF ORIGIN DULY CERTIFIED BY C.C.P.I.T. STATING THE NAME OF THE MANUFACTURERS OF PRODUCERS AND THAT GOODS EXPORTED ARE WHOLLY OF CHINESE ORIGIN.
		+ THE PRODUCTION DATE OF THE GOODS NOT TO BE EARLIER THAN HALF MONTH AT TIME OF SHIPMENT. BENEFICIARY MUST CERTIFY THE SAME.
		+ SHIPMENT TO BE EFFECTED BY CONTAINER AND BY REGULAR LINE.SHIPMENT COMPANY'S CERTIFICATE TO THIS EFFECT SHOULD ACCOMPANY THE DOCUMENTS.
		+ ONE COPY ISSUED OR ENDORSED TO THE ORDER OF ALRAJHI BANKING AND INVESTMENT CORP. FOR THE INVOICE PLUS TEN PERCENT COVERING ALL RISKS, INSTITUTE CARGO CLAUSES, INSTITUTE STRIKES.
DD. CONDITIONS	47 A	ADDITIONAL CONDITION
		A DISCREPANCY FEE OF USD50.00 WILL BE IMPOSED ON EACH SET OF DOCUMENTS PRESENTED FOR NEGOTIATION UNDER THIS L/C WITH DISCREPANCY. THE FEE WILL BE DEDUCTED FROM THE BILL AMOUNT.
CHARGES	71 B	ALL CHARGES AND COMMISSIONS OUTSIDE KSA WILL BE ON THE BENEFICIARIES' ACCOUNT INCLUDING REIMBURSING, BANK COMMISSION, DISCREPANCY FEE (IF ANY) AND COURIER CHARGES.
CONFIRMATION INSTR.	*49	WITHOUT
REIMBURS. BANK	53 D	/ /
		ALRAJHI BANKING AND INVESTMENT CORP. RIYADH (HEAD OFFICE)
INS.PAYING BANK	78	
		DOCUMENTS TO BE DESPATCHED IN ONE LOT BY COURIER ALL CORRESPONDENCE TO BE SENT TO ALRAJHI BANKING AND INVESTMENT COPRORATION RIYADH (HEAD OFFICE)
SEND REC. INFO.	72	REIMBURSEMENT IS SUBJECT TO ICC URR 525
TRAILER		ORDER IS <MAC:> <PAC:> <ENC:> <CHK:> <TNG:> <PDE:> MAC: E55927A4 CHK: 7B505952829A HOB:

<table>
<tr><td colspan="6">南京蓝星贸易公司
NANJING LANXING CO., LTD.
ROOM 2501, TIAN JIA MANSION, BEIJING WEST ROAD, NANJING 210005, P.R.CHINA
TEL: 025-84715004, 025-84715619 FAX: 025-84691619</td></tr>
<tr><td colspan="6">**COMMERCIAL INVOICE**</td></tr>
<tr><td rowspan="4">**To**</td><td colspan="2" rowspan="4">EAST AGENT COMPANY
3-72, OHTAMACHI, NAKA-KU,
YOKOHAMA, JAPAN</td><td>**Invoice No.**</td><td colspan="2">2009SDT009</td></tr>
<tr><td>**Invoice Date**</td><td colspan="2">August 12, 2009</td></tr>
<tr><td>**S/C No.**</td><td colspan="2">09TG28711</td></tr>
<tr><td>**S/C Date**</td><td colspan="2">JULY 22, 2009</td></tr>
<tr><td>**From**</td><td colspan="2">NANJING</td><td>**To**</td><td colspan="2">AKITA</td></tr>
<tr><td>**Letter of Credit No.**</td><td colspan="2">LTR0505457</td><td>**Date**</td><td colspan="2">090727</td></tr>
<tr><td>**Marks and Numbers**</td><td>Description of Goods</td><td>Quantity</td><td>Unit Price</td><td colspan="2">Amount</td></tr>
<tr><td>V.H
LAS PLAMS
C/NO.1-180</td><td>180 CARTONS
H6-59940BS
GOLF CAPS</td><td>1 800DOZS</td><td>CIF AKITA
USD 8.10</td><td colspan="2">USD 14 580.00</td></tr>
<tr><td></td><td>**TOTAL**</td><td>1 800 DOZS</td><td></td><td colspan="2">USD14 580.00</td></tr>
<tr><td colspan="4"></td><td colspan="2"></td></tr>
<tr><td>**SAY TOTAL**</td><td colspan="5">**SAY UNITED STATES DOLLARS FOURTEEN THOUSAND FIVE HUNDRED AND EIGHTY ONLY.**</td></tr>
</table>

<table>
<tr><td colspan="2">ISSUER
DALIAN ARTS & CRAFTS
IMPORT & EXPORT CORP.
NO. 23 FUGUI STR. DALIAN, CHINA</td><td colspan="3" rowspan="2">商业发票
COMMERCIAL INVOICE</td></tr>
<tr><td colspan="2" rowspan="2">TO
BELLAFLORA GARTEN CENTER
GESELLSCHAFT M. B. H.
FRANZOSENHAUSWEG 50
A-2040 LINZ</td></tr>
<tr><td>NO.
2009AC031</td><td colspan="2">DATE
June 2, 2009</td></tr>
<tr><td colspan="2" rowspan="2">TRANSPORT DETAILS
ANY PORT OF CHINA TO VIENNA</td><td>S/C NO.
No. 205001</td><td colspan="2">L/C NO.
372623</td></tr>
<tr><td colspan="3">TERMS OF PAYMENT
L/C AT SIGHT</td></tr>
<tr><td>Marks and Numbers</td><td>Description of Goods</td><td>Quantity</td><td>Unit Price</td><td>Amount</td></tr>
<tr><td></td><td>3 CARTONS

CHRISTMAS GIFTS
AG-1355
AG-1409A
AG-1409B
AG-1429
AG-1434
AG-1451
AG-1455
AG-1473
AG-1476
AG-1480
AG-1501
AG-1502
AG-1503
AG-1505
DL- (EACH 400 DOZ)
1556B, 1568B, 1571B,
1603B, 1637B,
1679B, 1691B, 1768B,
1770B, 1771B
DL-1734B
(EACH 400 DOZ)
DL-1846B, DL-1889B
AM-648
AM-3
C-32</td><td>(SETS)

768
1 600
600
768
1 600
600
672
420
382
240
900
648
840
960

(DOZ)
4 000
400
800
750 PCS
750 PCS
600 PCS</td><td>CIF VIENNA
(USD)

0.66
0.46
1.01
0.78
0.50
0.50
0.52
0.76
0.90
0.95
0.52
0.68
0.58
0.52

2.15
4.10
3.96
0.54
1.54
1.43</td><td>CIF VIENNA
(USD)

506.88
736.00
606.00
599.04
800.00
300.00
349.44
319.20
343.80
228.00
468.00
440.64
487.20
499.20

8 600.00
1 640.00
3 168.00
405.00
1,155.00
858.00</td></tr>
<tr><td></td><td>TOTAL</td><td></td><td></td><td>USD 22,509.40</td></tr>
<tr><td>SAY TOTAL</td><td colspan="4">SAY U.S.DOLLARS TWENTY TWO THOUSAND FIVE HUNDRED AND NINE POINT FOUR ONLY.</td></tr>
</table>

<table>
<tr><td colspan="2">Shipper
SHANGHAI TEXTILES
IMPORT & EXPORT
CORPORATION</td><td colspan="2" rowspan="5">B/L No. CSA1505

中国对外贸易运输总公司
上海 SHANGHAI
联 运 提 单
COMBINED TRANSPORT
BILL OF LADING
RECEIVED the goods in apparent good order and condition as specified below unless otherwise stated herein.
THE Carrier, in accordance with the provisions contained in this document,
1) undertakes to perform or to procure the performance of the entire transport from the place at which the goods are taken in charge to the place designated for delivery in this document, and
2) assumes liability as prescribed in this document for such transport. One of the Bills of Lading must be surrendered duty indorsed in exchange for the goods or delivery order.</td></tr>
<tr><td colspan="2">Consignee or order
CRYSTAL KOBE LTD.,
ROOM 300, 1410 BROADWAY,
NEW YORK, NY10018
U.S.A.</td></tr>
<tr><td colspan="2">Notify address
THE SAME AS CONSIGNEE
TEL NO.: 559-525-70000</td></tr>
<tr><td>Pre-carriage by</td><td>Place of receipt</td></tr>
<tr><td>Ocean vessel
ZHELU V.031118SE</td><td>Port of loading
SHANGHAI</td></tr>
<tr><td>Port of discharge
NEW YORK</td><td>Place of delivery</td><td>Freight payable at
SHANGHAI</td><td>Number of original Bs/L
THREE(3)</td></tr>
<tr><td colspan="4">Marks and Nos. Number and kind of packages Description of goods Gross weight(kgs.) Measurement(m^3)
CRYSTAL KOBE LTD., LADIES' 55% ACRYLIC 45% COTTON
NEW YORK KNITTED BLOUSE IN CARTON 2,548KGS 11.58M^3
ORDER NO. 21SSG-017 STYLE NO. H32331SE
STYLE NO. H32331SE 500 DOZ AT USD48.50 PER DOZ
L-02-I-03437 CIF NEW YORK LESS 3 PCT</td></tr>
<tr><td colspan="4">CARTON NO.1~120
MADE IN CHINA FREIGHT PREPAID
ABOVE PARTICULARS FURNISHED BY SHIPPER</td></tr>
<tr><td colspan="2" rowspan="4">Freight and charges</td><td colspan="2">IN WITNESS whereof the number of original Bills of Lading stated above have been signed, one of which being accomplished, the other(s) to be void.</td></tr>
<tr><td colspan="2">Place and date of issue
SHANGHAI Nov. 20, 2009</td></tr>
<tr><td>Signed for or on behalf of the carrier</td><td></td></tr>
<tr><td>WAN JIANPING AS AGENT
FOR THE CARRIER NAMED ABOVE</td><td></td></tr>
</table>

<table>
<tr><td colspan="2">Shipper
NANJING FOREIGN TRADE IMP. and EXP. CORP.</td><td colspan="3">B/L NO.</td></tr>
<tr><td colspan="2">Consignee or order
To ORDER</td><td colspan="3" rowspan="3">PIL
PACIFIC INTERNATIONAL LINES (PTE) LTD.
(Incorporated in Singapore)
COMBINED TRANSPORT BILL OF LADING
Received in apparent good order and condition except as otherwise noted the total number of container or other packages or units enumerated below for transportation from the place of receipt to the place of delivery subject to the terms hereof. One of the signed Bills of Lading must be surrendered duly endorsed in exchange for the Goods or delivery order. On presentation of this document (duly) Endorsed to the Carrier by or on behalf of the Holder, the rights and liabilities arising in accordance with the terms hereof shall (without prejudice to any rule of common law or statute rendering them binding on the Merchant) become binding in all respects between the Carrier and the Holder as though the contract evidenced hereby had been made between them.
SEE TERMS ON ORIGINAL B/L</td></tr>
<tr><td colspan="2">Notify Party</td></tr>
<tr><td colspan="2">EAST AGENT COMPANY, 126 Rome Street, Antwerp, Belgium</td></tr>
<tr><td>Vessel and Voyage Number</td><td>Port of Loading</td><td colspan="3">Port of Discharge</td></tr>
<tr><td>DAFENG E002</td><td>NANJING</td><td colspan="3">LONDON</td></tr>
<tr><td>Place of Receipt</td><td>Place of Delivery</td><td colspan="3">Number of Original Bs/L</td></tr>
<tr><td>NANJING</td><td></td><td colspan="3">THREE（3）</td></tr>
<tr><td colspan="5">PARTICULARS AS DECLARED BY SHIPPER-CARRIER NOT RESPONSIBLE</td></tr>
<tr><td>Container Nos/Seal Nos. Marks and Numbers</td><td colspan="2">No. of Container / Packages / Description of Goods</td><td>Gross Weight (Kilos)</td><td>Measurement (cu. meters)</td></tr>
<tr><td>CBD
LONDON
NOS1-200

200 CARTONS</td><td colspan="2">LADIES' LYCRA LONG PANT
2,400 PIECES
USD20.00 CIF LONDON
12 PIECES TO A CARTON

CLEAN ON BOARD</td><td>2,000KGS</td><td>6 M^3</td></tr>
<tr><td>FREIGHT & CHARGES</td><td colspan="4">Number of Containers/Packages (in words)</td></tr>
<tr><td rowspan="3">FREIGHT PREPAID</td><td colspan="4">SAY TWO HUNDRED CARTONS ONLY
Shipped on Board Date
OCTOBER 20, 2008
Place and Date of Issue
NANJING</td></tr>
<tr><td colspan="4">In Witness whereof this number of original Bills of Lading stated above all of the tenor and date one of which being accomplished, the others to stand void.</td></tr>
<tr><td colspan="4">for PACIFIC INTERNATIONAL LINES (PTE) LTD. as Carrier</td></tr>
</table>

中国人民保险公司
THE PEOPLE'S INSURANCE COMPANY OF CHINA

总公司设于北京 一九四九年创立
Head Office: BEIJING Established in 1949

保险单 号次
INSURANCE POLICY No. SH01/0456980

中国人民保险公司（以下简称本公司）
This Policy of Insurance witnesses that The People's Insurance Company of China (hereinafter called
根据上海市纺织品进出口有限公司
"the Company"), at the request of SHANGHAI TEXTILES IMP. & EXP. CORP.
（以下简称被保险人）的要求，由被保险人向本公司缴付约定
(hereinafter called "the Insured") and in consideration of the agreed premium paid to the Company
的保险费，按照本保险单承保险别和背面所载条款与下列
by the Insured, undertakes to insure the undermentioned goods in transportation subject to the conditions
条款承保下述货物运输保险，特立本保险单。
of this Policy as per the Clause printed overleaf and other special clauses attached hereon.

标 记 Marks & Nos.	包装及数量 Quantity	保险货物项目 Description of Goods	保险金额 Amount Insured
As per Invoice No. STP015088	120 CARTONS	LADIES' 55% ACRYLIC 45% COTTON KNITTED BLOUSE	USD 26 675.00

总保险金额：
Total Amount Insured: SAY US DOLLARS TWENTY SIX THOUSAND SIX HUNDRED AND SEVENTY FIVE ONLY

保 费 费率 装载运输工具
Premium: as arranged Rate as arranged Per conveyance S.S. ZHE LU V.031118SE

开航日期 自 至
Slg.on or abt. As Per B/L From SHANGHAI to NEW YORK

承保险别
Conditions
COVERING ALL RISKS, WAR RISK AS PER THE RELEVANT OCEAN MARINE CARGO CLAUSE OF P.I.C.C. DATED JAN.1, 1981.

所保货物，如遇出险，本公司凭本保险单及其他有关证件给付赔款。
Claims, if any, payable on surrender of this Policy together with other relevant documents.
所保货物，如发生本保险单项下负责赔偿的损失或事故，
In the event of accident whereby loss or damage may result in a claim under this Policy immediate
应立即通知本公司下述代理人查勘。
notice applying for survey must be given to the Company's Agent as mentioned hereunder:
赔款偿付地点
Claim payable at NEW YORK

日期
Date Nov. 18, 2009
地址：中国上海中山东一路27号
Address: 27 Zhongshan Dong Yi Lu Shanghai, China.
Cables: 42001 Shanghai.
Telex: 33128 PICCS CN

中国人民保险公司上海分公司
THE PEOPLE'S INSURANCE CO. OF CHINA
SHANGHAI BRANCH

General Manager

上海市纺织品进出口有限公司

SHANGHAI TEXTILES I/E CORP.

PACKING LIST

ADDRESS: 27, ZHONGSHAN ROAD E.1.

TEL: 86-21-65342517 FAX: 86-21-65124743

MESSRS:
CRYSTAL KOBE LTD.,
1410 BROADWAY, ROOM 3000
NEW YORK, N.Y. 10018 U.S.A.

INVOICE NO.: STP015088
S/C NO.: 21SSG-017
Date: NOV. 8, 2009

DESCRIPTION OF GOODS	SHIPPING MARKS
55% ACRYLIC 45% COTTON LADIES' KNITTED BLOUSE STYLE NO. H32331SE PAYMENT BY L/C NO. L-02-I-03437 SHIPPING S/C NO.	CRYSTAL KOBE LTD., NEW YORK ORDER NO. 21SSG-017 STYLE NO. H32331SE L-02-I-03437 CARTON NO.1~120 MADE IN CHINA

COLOUR BREAKDOWN		SIZE							
COLOR		PACK	S	M	L	XL	XXL	XXXL	TOTAL(PCS)
IVORY			120	360	240				720
BLACK			320	360	440				1 120
NAVYBLUE			180	180	100				460
RED			432	580	440				1 452
WHITE			78	234	156				468
BROWN			160	280	220				660
TAWNY			320	360	440				1 120
TOTAL(PCS):									6 000

		SIZE ASSORTMENT							QUANTITY
CTN NO.	COLOR	CTNS	S	M	L	XL	XXL	XXXL	(PCS)
1~20	IVORY	20	6	18	12				720
21~40	BLACK	20	16	18	22				1 120
41~50	NAVYBLUE	10	18	18	10				460
51~66	RED	16	16	28	22				1 056
67~79	WHITE	13	6	18	12				468
80~89	BROWN	10	16	28	22				660
90~109	TAWNY	20	16	18	22				1 120
110~120	RED	11	16	12	8				396
TOTAL:	6 000 PCS IN 120 CARTONS ONLY								

GROSS WT.:	2 584 KGS	NET WT.:	2 326KGS
MEASUREMENT:	60×40×40CBM		11.58CBM

For and on behalf of
上海市纺织品进出口有限公司
SHANGHAI TEXTILES I/E CORP.

Authorized Signature(s)

SHANGHAI TEXTILES IMPORT & EXPORT CORPORATION

27 ZHONGSHAN ROAD E.1.
SHANGHAI CHINA
TEL: 86-21-65342517 FAX: 86-21-65124743

SHIPPING ADVICE

Nov. 20, 2009

Messrs: **CRYSTAL KOBE LTD.**
Dear Sirs:

Re: **Invoice No.: STP015088** **L/C No.: L-02-I-03437**

We hereby inform you that the goods under the above mentioned credit have been shipped. The details of the shipment as stated below.

Commodity: **LADIES' 55% ACRYLIC 45% COTTON KNITTED BLOUSE**

Quantity: **120 CARTONS**

Amount: **USD 23 522.50**

Ocean Vessel: **ZHELU V.031118SE**

Bill of Lading No.: **CSA1505**

E.T.D.: **On / or about Nov.25, 2009**

Port of Loading: **SHANGHAI**

Destination: **NEW YORK**

We hereby certify that the above content is true and correct.

SHANGHAI TEXTILES IMPORT & EXPORT CORP.

× × ×

References

甘鸿．1996．外经贸英语函电．上海：上海科学技术文献出版社．

江运芳．2007．外贸英语函电．重庆：重庆大学出版社．

兰天．2004．外贸英语函电．5 版．大连：东北财经大学出版社．

刘慧侠．2004．外贸函电．北京：科学出版社．

孟建国．2009．外贸英语函电．杭州：浙江大学出版社．

毅冰．2012．十天搞定外贸函电．北京：中国海关出版社．

祝卫．2008．出口贸易模拟操作教程．3 版．上海：上海人民出版社．